HOW
CHILDHOOD HARDSHIP
PREPARED me for LIFE

By
Chagai Chol Lual
Founder of Padang Lutheran Christian Relief

PADANG LUTHERAN CHRISTIAN RELIEF
www.plcr.org

Partial proceeds from the sale of this book
will be donated to Padang Lutheran
Christian Relief in order to support its relief
efforts on the ground in Southern Sudan.

Order this book online at www.trafford.com/09-0042
or email orders@trafford.com

Most Trafford titles are also available at major online book retailers.

Editor: Tom Lee, Eveready Press, New Westminster, BC.

Note for Librarians: A cataloguing record for this book is available from Library
and Archives Canada at www.collectionscanada.ca/amicus/index-e.html

Printed in Victoria, BC, Canada.

ISBN: 978-1-4269-0147-8

*We at Trafford believe that it is the responsibility of us all, as both individuals
and corporations, to make choices that are environmentally and socially sound.
You, in turn, are supporting this responsible conduct each time you purchase a
Trafford book, or make use of our publishing services. To find out how you are
helping, please visit www.trafford.com/responsiblepublishing.html*

*Our mission is to efficiently provide the world's finest, most comprehensive
book publishing service, enabling every author to experience success.
To find out how to publish your book, your way, and have it available
worldwide, visit us online at www.trafford.com/10510*

www.trafford.com

North America & international
toll-free: 1 888 232 4444 (USA & Canada)
phone: 250 383 6864 ♦ fax: 250 383 6804
email: info@trafford.com

The United Kingdom & Europe
phone: +44 (0)1865 487 395 ♦ local rate: 0845 230 9601
facsimile: +44 (0)1865 481 507 ♦ email: info.uk@trafford.com

10 9 8 7 6 5 4 3 2

DEDICATION

IT IS AN HONOUR TO DEDICATE THIS BOOK TO

My mother, Nyanbuny Ayuel Koryom
and my half-brother, Dhieu Kiir Lual.

TO BERNICE FINDLAY

Chagai Lual

June 19, 2009

CONTENTS

FOREWORD

I decided to write this book to share my life story with my children, an endeavor that has taken one year to complete. I have told my story as accurately as possible. The circumstances and emotional hardships I have experienced are miserably comparable to that of many orphans around the globe. I would hope that the readers could learn about enduring circumstances and depression that I had faced during my childhood with my single mother and siblings. In some ways, someone with the same understanding may recognize and remember my story in a different way. In other ways, the story is mine and for that I ask forgiveness. Read, learn and enjoy!

Chagai Chol Lual
Vancouver, BC, Canada
March 2009

FOR BERNICE FINDLAY

Chul

chagai Lual

June 19, 2009

ACKNOWLEDGMENTS

First and foremost I would like to praise my mother, Nyanbuny Ayuel Koryom for her tireless hard work and support in raising me with my siblings during the terrible hardship. Her devoted parenting and guidance have inspired me. I would like to thank my sisters, Areng, Nyanyiik and my younger brother Dhot, as well as my cousin Angui Dau Chol for their absolute love and confidence in me and all my deeds. My honest gratitude goes to my dear half-brother Dhieu Kiir Lual for his efforts to put me through school and I commend him for persuading me to pursue my education. I am very grateful to my half-brother Monytong Wuor Lual and the entire Lual Kiir Arieu family for their care and prayers for my well-being. I am extremely grateful to my friend Chigai Miyom Wuor for being a truthful friend and for continuing to be a devoted friend. I am thankful to Ahol Awan Arop for being more generous to me than some of my own relatives. I also want to extend my thanks to Bol Machol Jok for his terrific support and advice in the refugee camp in Ethiopia. His guidance was valuable and helpful.

I would like to thank my friend Deng Mabil Awuol for being like my blood brother. Moreover, I want to express in particular my enormous thanks to Agei Deng Malek for being amazingly honest and supportive. My sincere thank to Rev. Lexson Awad Maku for your kindhearted support to everyone. In addition, I would like to convey my immense gratitude to Rev. Marlys Moen for all her support and good counsel. Her willingness to assist and expertise helped enormously in shaping this manuscript. My heartfelt thanks also goes to my friends in my second homeland in Canada, especially Judy Kochendorfer who has been teaching the ESL class at Mount Zion Lutheran Church, as well as Dr. Bruce Cornish and Geroline Vitcoe for their faithful friendships and diligent endeavors to help many immigrants improve their English and enjoy their time in Canada. Their regular commitment and hard work enables many immigrants to assimilate rapidly and strengthen their use of English skills. I am absolutely indebted to Art Birzneck and the entire Birzneck family for everything. My deepest thanks to Stephen Scheving for his thoughtfulness to the less fortune people in Sudan. I am particularly thankful to the entire congregation of Mount Zion Lutheran Church for their warm welcome and support for the people of Southern Sudan at their Church. I also want to thank Tom Lee from Eveready Press for editing this manuscript.

My sincere thank also goes to the dedicated teams from Trafford Publishing for their diligence to speed the book for publication. Finally, I would like to thank my loving wife, Aluel Deng Nyok for her continuous support and encouragement. I would like to thank my dear sons, Kiir, Lual and my lovely daughter, Arop for their love, patience and understanding during the writing of this book.

Furthermore, I would like to ask for forgiveness to those whose names are not mentioned in this manuscript. Rest assured that you will always remain in my memory.

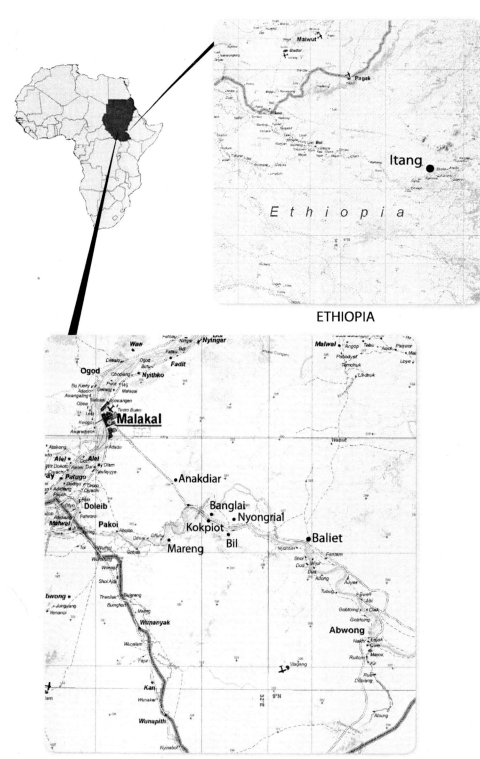

ETHIOPIA

UPPER NILE STATE, SUDAN

Chapter 1

BACKGROUND AND EARLY CHILDHOOD

I was born in 1972 in Ajuba remote area, now known as Nyongrial Locality, thirty miles southeast of Malakal in Southern Sudan. I used the word "year" without a tangible date and month because my mother was illiterate, so she did not know the exact date of my birth. Life was particularly primitive thus the children who were delivered by Traditional Birthing Attandants have no documents such as birth certificates and immunization records in those days. In such situations, dates were linked with events to memorize the year in which you were born, like the year of a famine or war. My mother remembered the year of my birth because of the Addis Ababa Peace Agreement which was signed in 1972 between the Khartoum military regime of President Jaffer Numeir and the Southern Sudan Liberation Movement better known as Anya-anya one.

Sadly, my father died a few weeks before my birth, leaving my mother with a young hungry family to look after. However, the year of my birth was actually the year of grief for my mother who had buried her beloved husband and three children earlier. This is reflected in my name Chagai, a word in the Dinka language for someone who has gone through awful sorrow.

There was neither a medical doctor nor a trained midwife to help deliver the babies in the area but my mother told me that I was delivered with the help of my maternal grandmother, Arop Monyjok Reth, who was the traditional birthing attendant in our village. I was born at home like other babies at that time in a traditional mud hut with a grass thatched roof with nothing in it except for a few cowhide skins to sleep on. There was no baby crib or diapers, let alone vaccinations or toys during those days.

My elder sister, Areng Chol Lual, was the last sibling to see my father alive, but I never knew what it was like to have a father around. As mentioned at the onset, I was one of the luckless children on earth to live without both parents since the first day of my birth. In Dinka society, when you have lost one of your parents, you are considered an orphan, even if one of your parents is still alive. Although I did not enjoy having a father throughout my life I am now doing everything I can to ensure that my children experience a different life, because I want to provide them with a stable upbringing, something I missed.

My mother started in farming and went on relief to keep us alive after I was born. She just managed to make ends meet by working like a slave for the meager reward (called Awur in Dinka) to put food on the table for her children. She would trudge to the grassy fields daily during the severe winters to reap and winnow the crops in the fields of the local rich people in exchange for food rations. Her tireless hard work helped us all through hard times. Even though my mother was working hard, our life was a recurring struggle.

I still recall the glance of my mother when we were hungry and desperate. As we barely had anything to eat, so we would resort to eating a handful of sediment that my mother would collect from the traditional homemade wine brewers in the Ajuba area. In the Dinka language we called it Athuai. In addition, my mother would gather certain types of plants for food and I became absolutely delighted by how little one needed to survive. Given the fact that I was raised by a single mother who relied at times on food for work, I really appreciated the effort of those who offered this kind of work to create job opportunities for other vulnerable people in the community. These experiences helped me understand the pain that my mother had often expressed as I was growing up to learn that I can realize my own dreams through hard work and then give back to our community through volunteering my time. When there was nothing to eat then my mother would assure us about it and I would know that our little food ration had run out because she never told a lie in her life. All these experiences have motivated me with a very strong passion in my heart to help those most in need around me and beyond.

My late maternal grandmother Arop Monyjok Reth

would farm in her sorghum field despite her old age in order to support us. She graciously gave us a milking cow to drink its milk and I appreciated this gift because otherwise we would have been without milk. This cow provided us daily milk until it was stolen by the Shilluk bandits in 1985 in the cattle camp in the lakeshore in the Shilluk Kingdom after I left it with other cows in Wuol village while I was sick. This was the start of the tribal conflicts between the Shilluk and the Dinka tribes.

My maternal aunt Akon Ayuel Koryom used to assist my mother in raising us during those difficult times, even though she was a true widow like my mother and struggled for her own needs and that of her children. My maternal grandmother Arop Monyjok Reth and my maternal aunt Akon Ayuel Koryom died when I was in the refugee camp in Ethiopia.

I still fall asleep with all their images in my mind. There were no family photos in our home during those days. Even now, my mother still can't look at the pictures. My mother is a remarkable woman, the elder daughter of two children of Arop Monyjok Reth and Ayuel Koryom Deng. My mother has ability to find humor in almost any situation. Being a mother was the most important job of her life. She had enough love to go around for her children.

Her only sister Akon Ayuel Koryom passed away in 1991 just a year after the death of her mother Arop Monyjok Reth in 1990. She wondered how she had survived the usual childhood illnesses while so many of her siblings did not and she struggled with the difficulties that shaped her life.

As I have mentioned, I was brought up in one of the luckless families who did not benefited from others. My mother Nyanbuny Ayuel Koryom was a widow and my late maternal aunt Akon Ayuel Koryom was a widow. In addition, my late paternal grandmother Adau Koth and my late maternal grandmother Arop Monyjok Reth were both widows. Beside that, my late father Chol Lual Kiir lost his father Lual Kiir Arieu when he was still young, so he did not benefit from having his father either. Presently, my elder sister Areng Chol Lual is a widow.

During the initiation of my father Chol Lual Kiir into

adulthood, he was given the gift of a spear for dancing by his half brother Wuor Lual Kiir. Actually, the half brothers of my late father were more supportive than my own half brothers of which some are self-centeredness.

My mother was clearly an enormous influence on my life through her sheer determination and perseverance for me to survive. As a child, I desperately wanted to know where my father was and I often asked my mother about that.

I endured hardships in my childhood and my mother endured hardships in her life because she was widowed with children in her middle age. Throughout my childhood my mother taught me to overcome ordeals by hopefulness, a lesson that prepared me for later in life. My mother would awake in the early morning and head off to the field where she would spend the whole day reaping the crops. She sometimes left me with my younger sister Nyanyiik to baby-sit for hours in a day. I used to carry my six months old sister Nyanyiik on my back as I walked ten miles to reach my mother in the field so that she could breast-feed the baby. My younger sister Nyanyiik now has two children of her own. My mother was working hard under the sun for the sake of her children.

Being the elder son, I took the responsibility as breadwinner of our family at the age of fourteen. As well, being raised by a single mother I was often fretful about having something to eat with my siblings and our mother. I was actually eager to work hard due to the fact that I was growing up without a father. The few times I asked my mother about the whereabouts of my father, she would respond by singing the traditional songs of my father and then she would sob. I also learned to work very hard in order to please the merciless men around me. My hard work was appreciated by many men who were around me. Some of those men used to be jealous of my work and would say to their own sons to work hard like me. I thought that some of those fathers might have wished that I was their own son and that made me feel proud and delighted.

My mother loved me and wanted me to stay alive because she knew that I had strong shoulders and would take responsibility for my siblings when I grew up.

My father Chol Lual Kiir was a cattle keeper and farmed full time. He was also one of the best traditional dancers in Ajuba area. My mother Nyanbuny Ayuel Koryom was a farmer like many ordinary people in the area. This was sensible work for a single mother with four children to feed. Moreover, my mother was a voluntary traditional birth attendant who spent many, many years helping with deliveries for women in the remote area of Ajuba district. She was famous for the number of healthy babies that she had been able to help deliver into the world.

I am a Dinka by tribe from Padang community and my clan is Ngok Lual Yak. Everyone in Baliet County is from the Ngok Lual Yak and Dongjol clans. Baliet County has only Dinka citizens but Malakal is a mixed city with Dinka the largest tribe present there. I was raised and grew up in Ajuba area which is the richest farming community in Baliet County. My late father, Chol Lual Kiir was from Ajuba section and my mother, Nyanbuny Ayuel Koryom, is from Baliet Kunam section or Baliet Panyaldior as people call it.

My paternal grandfather Lual Kiir Arieu was from Ajuba section. My paternal grandmother Adau Koth was from Thoi clan while my maternal grandmother Arop Monyjok Reth was from Baliet Pajuac section, but all of them were from Ngok Lual Yak clan except my paternal grandmother Adau Koth who was from Thoi clan. Thoi is part of Padang which united thirteen clans including Ngok Lual Yak. However, my parents were from Dinka Ngok Lual Yak clan and my great grandfather Kiir Arieu Ngor was originally said to have come from Adong section where we still maintain family links with the family of Mabek Ngor. My paternal grandfather Lual Kiir Arieu was a traditional chief in our village who was involved in tribal traditional court by settling local disputes about marriages and cows.

I was the fifth born of nine among my mother's children, although five of them died young so only four of us survived two girls and two boys. I am the second surviving child and the eldest son in our family. According to my mother she said that

I had survived against all odds at the early age after the deaths of five of my siblings, two of whom I baby-sat. When you have survived in your childhood, you have survived in a special way with wonderful memories and I credited the traumatic events of my childhood for my clear memory of that time. My sister Nyanyiik was born in 1976 and my youngest brother Dhot was born in 1978. When my brother Dhot was younger he had bad humor, but, of course, family life settled him down. I think he might have taken this bad humor from my half brother Dol Kiir Lual. At summer, my late maternal grandmother Arop Monyjok Reth would take me to Wune Kuanynok village to stay with her and we would go out planting.

My father was the first born and the only son among two sisters of his mother Adau Koth and he was also the only son of Lual Kiir Arieu, from his second wife Adau Koth. My relatives said that my father was loved in Ajuba as much for his generosity and influence as for his songs and dancing. He was so inspirational to the people about sharing and helping the less fortune people in his community. My relatives said that my father would put the needs of his community before his own and did what he thought was right despite any personal cost. To keep the legacy of my father alive, I was overwhelmed by the elders in the greater Ajuba area who would come to me while they were a little drunk and tell me how great my father was. It was the first time it even occurred to me that my father even had a life in Ajuba area before all of us. So it was kind of a wake-up call for me to follow in the footsteps of my late father. My father was the best singer and traditional dancer in the Ajuba area where his friends and relatives said he would sing and dance with the attractive girls in Ajuba and Kunam areas, where he probably would have met my mother. My father kept his dancing activities until his death. My mother also continually praised my father whom she said was a great man of his word and deed. At nights, my mother would sing the songs of my father and sometimes she might still be singing before falling asleep. While my mother sang I would listen as much to the songs she sang as to the beautiful melody coming from her voice. My mother instilled in four of her children a great love of the dancing songs of my father. The dancing lessons she taught me gave me more interest at an early age to follow in the footsteps of my father as a dancer. Should it not have been for the case of the so-called school and civil war that displaced me, I would have been a great dancer in my area at the moment, but my half brother Dhieu Kiir Lual told me to go to school instead.

As mentioned previously, my mother taught me how to sing the traditional songs of my late father at an early age. My earliest memories were of singing the dancing songs of my father when I was about nine years old. When I first sang the dancing songs of my late father with the loud voice, my mother cried and hugged me really tight and I couldn't figure out why she was too joyful with this.

I still sing the traditional songs of my late father. In addition, my relatives and neighbors are still memorizing the songs of my late father Chol Lual Kiir in Ajuba area. Wherever the people sing the songs of my late father, the women of my paternal relations would weep and trill.

My late maternal grandmother Arop made you feel at home with her incredible cooking and her gleaming eyes. She was a very quiet woman, excluding the time after she had sipped the traditional wine and become somewhat talkative. She loved to sing the Dinka traditional praising songs but she had a very terrible voice. As the elder son, my mother wanted me to become a dancer to follow in the footsteps of my late father. I had always been good and obedient toward my mother since childhood and I was very excited with her suggestion and advice.

RURAL LIFE IN SOUTHERN SUDAN

I spent my early life in the Ajuba area until the second civil war broke out in 1983 between the North and the South. Before the civil war, life was what it was meant to be given the new lease on life with the Addis Ababa Agreement which was signed in 1972 to end the first Sudanese civil war. In the time of my childhood, my mother lived, and is still living, in a very small grass thatched hut without running water or electricity. We lived in the traditional mud hut with a grass thatched roof as huge as most North American bathrooms. It was a very comfortable house by Dinka standards, like other houses in the village. We shared this house with goats, chickens, sheep and dogs. The dogs often bark at night time. For furniture, we used to sleep on the cow hides or slept on the bare floor full of insects. There were neither dinner tables nor chairs so we would sit on the ground to eat our meals. There was neither electricity nor running water in our village. There was no toilet or shower in our house which was not strange in those days to the present. For these reasons, we would proceed outside to the forest to relieve ourselves there. We used to bath in the river or nearby stream. We would frequently bath in the river or stream possibly three times per month in the winter. I had never seen a light bulb or the noise of traffic until the age of about fifteen years old in Malakal.

As a child, I used to gather eggs secretly from under clucking hens and eat them with other children. My mother cooked food in an iron pot over an open fire in front of our hut or inside our hut during the rain by using firewood. Everything we ate was grown in our own fields. We planted maize and sorghum in our field where we took advantage of the rain when it came and we raised livestock. We walked miles in the dry season to fetch water.

As a child, I used to herd cattle in the bush with other boys of my age and we used to eat mud and drank water in the pool. I would get up long before dawn and open the cattle pen for the animals to head to the open pasture in Ajuba area. The boys would spend the day herding cattle while the girls enjoyed doing things together in the kitchen with their mothers and the likes. In Dinka culture, boys were taught the traditional trades such as hunting, fishing and herding cattle by their fathers or uncles while the girls were taught at an early age by their mothers and aunts about things concerning the household work to learn more about the traditional way of life. The women and girls would grind the grains and prepare the food for the family together in the houses. They would cook the food with metal pots and use to mix it with the cow cheese and sour milk.

In the evening, family members sat around the fire to warm themselves in the compound and the children listened to all kinds of stories from the adults and commit them to memory. As you grew up and assumed the position of the storyteller, you were able to retell these stories to your children or others in the village where animals roared and singing frogs croaked close by.

The crops were stored in the barn at home or in the field. Winter months were cold and the days were short. During the summer, there were continuous billowing rain clouds across the sky. Intermittently, the clouds dropped a lot of water on your head, and then the wind would come and dry you off. A beautiful rainbow followed as the sun appeared through the clouds. These rainbows occasionally lasted for hours, fading in and out as the sun shone through the clouds. Droughts and famine were so common and still are in many parts of Southern Sudan where most of the populations depend on agriculture. Community life in my extended family was like that of most people of modest means and I grew up in the remote area where life revolved around the evening meals and listening to the stories from the elders. There were many things that we did not have, yet we were always very happy with the little we had.

My adoring mother, maternal aunt and maternal grandmother were both committed traditional believers (animists) who took their traditional beliefs seriously. For this reason, we were taught about the importance of our family spirits and ancestors at an early age. Therefore, the family never celebrates Christmas as the birth of Jesus Christ because they were not aware that Jesus Christ was the son of God. The Arop Monyjok daughters dealt with the situation by sticking together closely. Sometimes we would live in the house of my maternal grandmother Arop Monyjok Reth and the three families would take the major meal together in the evening where they would sit on the ground and eat from one traditional dish under the clear moon. We called it "aduok" in Dinka language. The food was mixed with cows' butter and sour milk, something I enjoyed in my early childhood. However, I was perpetually restless and bothered. There was so much I did not appreciate and some of what I had learned, like the death of my father, had left me bitter and frustrated. I knew suffering at an early age from the little I had experienced with my family. In my childhood, I did not have three meals per day like other children in Southern Sudan where I was brought up.

My life on the farm before the second civil war prepared me for living under difficult conditions and I credited my mother for her love. Our mother was definitely the driving force for us during those days and she often advised us that if much is given then much is required. I never forgot that as I went on to live in various refugee camps. I always knew I needed to give something back.

In most Dinka culture, it was the work of women to winnow the freshly harvested ears of sorghum. My mother would winnow the crops in the fields. She would carry a sack of grain to the fields and spread the large mat made of leaves from the grass swamp on to the ground. Then she would wait for a strong wind to shake the grain in the batch from a large mat. The small birds would arrive to eat any spoils. As a teen without a father around, I used to help my mother all the way through all types of things such as reaping and driving away birds in the field. There was no paved road or vehicle of any kind. The ordinary people used to travel on foot and carry the crops and other food supplies on their heads like prisoners. Their burdens were balanced on their heads.

Many people of all tribes in greater Upper Nile State were able to come from a long distance for medical care in Malakal. Today, many people are still walking barefoot and tolerate many diseases without medical attention in Southern Sudan. In addition, most people still rely heavily on traditional healers and divination.

When I was seven years old, my maternal grandmother Arop Monyjok took me to Wune Kuanynok to stay with her. She was living in a very small grass thatched hut with neither electricity nor running water. It was a decorated traditional hut that she was very proud of, but a hut only the size of a small dog house in North America. My late grandmother Arop Monyjok was the absolute power in the family. Her words were law and none of her two daughters would ever challenge or disobey her. My maternal grandmother was a very significant source of information about our family history. She was the person whom I could ask many questions and if I did not ask her, she would relate many kinds of stories to me, as part of the traditional training to commit to memory. My maternal grandmother Arop loved the traditional home-made wine and seemed to be overjoyed every time she sat down and sip a gourd of it and become rather talkative. She loved to sing the traditional praising songs, but she had a very terrible voice that disturbed her neighbors.

When I was in Wune kunaynok, I used to play in the backyard with the children of my late maternal grandfather Aben Monyjok Reth in Wune Kuanynok village. We often sat on the dirty floor for hours playing with the mud that we made into cows with our bare hands. We would grab whatever we could to play with because there were no toys during those days in Southern Sudan. All these children who used to play with me have passed away one by one before they barely grew into adulthood.

I often played with these children until sunset when my maternal grandmother would roar with her terrible voice in Dinka language: "Dongwei Nyanbuny ja ben bei piny acie cuol" which means "Son of Nyanbuny, come home because it is already night time." As soon as I arrived in the house, I would grab the gourd full of sour milk and drink freely like a king, because I was the only child in the house with my maternal grandmother who loved me more than life. I wished this lovely old woman were still alive to benefit from the lessons she had taught me. After that, I would sit beside my maternal grandmother and she would pass on the things she felt were important for me to know. She told me that it was better to be poor than to have no friends. Being with the elders, I learned things about endurance and my concern for other people became as enormous as concern for myself. I learned a great deal from my grandmother.

She taught me how to tolerate and how to be patient.

I also used to go to Awier area to stay there with my aunt Akon Ayuel Koryom. I babysat three of the children of my aunt Akon Ayuel Koryom who had passed away. My beloved aunt Akon had been so thoughtful and generous to me. Traditionally, Dinka parents care deeply for their children and children care deeply for their parents throughout their old age. In the dusty village, children used to play in pools of muddy water and old women swept their homes while the elder men lazed on the dirty floor to discuss the harvest crop.

In Dinka culture, elderly people are treated with dignity and the place in the family unit is typically chosen for them. Elders are the most needed people because of their information and direction and many Dinka still hold tightly to traditional standards of conduct and decency.

MOURNING MY SIBLINGS FROM AN EARLY AGE

The human loss I have experienced is immense. As mentioned previously, my father died a few weeks before my birth and two of my younger sisters died when I was about seven years old. As a child, I used to ask my mother about the whereabouts of my father before I knew the meaning of the death. I still recall the day when my mother told me that my sister Nyanwach was dead. I went into shock and I did not weep. I even fell asleep at her funeral. My mother told me that she knew that this kind of sleep is a sign of extreme anxiety. In 1986, my youngest sister Nyanaben die and I remained with two sisters and one brother.

I experienced loss since the early days of my birth and I survived the odds that almost killed me. As always, I yearned to know why God let my father Chol Lual Kiir die while other men of his age were still alive to nurture their own children. I came up with no response after that from my mother who would often cry when I inquired about this issue. I felt hopeless and desperate to make these thoughts in my mind go away. I wished my father had cuddled me like most of the lucky children in my village who were used to enjoying an embrace from their fathers. Being an orphan in my community was one of the most distressing things in life, and I thought that I was the only orphan in the world who had no father. I was also angry with God for the misfortune I experienced within my own community. My mother kept praying to her family spirits about the health of our family and my health because my mother loved me more than life. Our relatives, particularly the elders who are no longer alive, were the ones who predicted that I would support all the relatives when I become a man. They used to advise my mother and encourage her that your son would help the relatives and others in the future.

To date, the prediction of my deceased relatives seems to be taking place as I am now engaged in many projects to help the poor in Sudan.

Chagai Chol Lual

Chapter 2

DINKA CUSTOMS AND CULTURAL BELIEFS

Before the civil war, the Dinka were living peacefully in the permanent villages of their ancestors but traveled in family groups to live in transitory homesteads with their cattle. The homesteads might be in clusters of one or two of each and every one in the groups. The Dinka were divided into more tribal groups which were further separated into clans, each occupying a territory of land large enough to supply water and grazing land for their herds. The villages were led by the traditional chief elected by the assembly. Traditional homes were made of mud walls with thatched grass in the roofs which might last about two years. Only women and children slept inside the house while the men slept in the mud-roofed cattle byre. The homesteads were located to enable movement in a range allowing year-around access to grass and water. Permanent villages were built on higher ground above the flood plain of the Nile River but with good water for irrigation.

The women and older men tended crops on this high ground while younger men moved up and down with the rise and fall of the river. Marriage was a necessity in the Dinka culture and polygamy was the ultimate for the Dinka. Men have as many wives as they can afford though many men may have only one wife at the moment. Every adult male was expected to raise a family and can marry as many wives as possible. Relatives also used to arrange for marriage to the ghost of a male who had died without getting marriage. Incest was usually unimaginable and, indeed, it is abhorred.

Dinka women kneel down before their husbands as they serve them the meal. The Dinka can marry outside their clan which promotes additional unity across the broader Dinka alliance as well as from other tribes.

The Dinka is a group of numerous, closely connected peoples living in areas along the countless streams and rivers concentrated in the greater Upper Nile and Bahr el Ghzal states in Southern Sudan. The Dinka is the initial principal tribal group in Southern Sudan followed by the Nuer tribe. The Dinka tribe retains the traditional rural life of the Nilotics but has additional crop growing in countless areas, growing grains, sorghum and maize as well as other crops.

In most of the Dinka clans, it was the work of women to do most of the household work and winnow the freshly harvested ears of sorghum but men do the farming and clear the forest for crop-growing sites. Girls learn to cook but boys do not. Cooking is done outdoors in the pots over a stone hearth. In Dinka traditions, a man must not cook or be near women as they cook. Men depend upon women for cooking their food and collecting fire wood as well as fetching drinking water in the stream during the dry season while the men were fishing, herding cattle and the periodic hunting of animals for food. A gentleman should not complain about hunger or starvation in Dinka society.

In Dinka traditions, the initiation into the adulthood is achieved through two means and procedures. The first step for Dinka people is to remove the six lower canines as a sign of maturity for children of both sexes. The second step is to initiate the boy into adulthood which is usually done by cutting six parallel lines across the forehead, a rite undertaken among boys of the same age. Initiation represents the formal inclusion of a male into society. It is not just an operational procedure but a painful and complicated ritual in preparation for manhood. In Dinka culture, an uninitiated man can not own a bull or preside in tribal ritual because he is considered by the entire community as a boy. After the initiation ceremony, the initiated man would be ready to marry or have a say in the family gathering which an uninitiated man could not dream of. But without the initiation, women would not be able to salute you as a man or kneel down before you as a sign of traditional respect while they are bringing you the food. After the initiation, the man would identify one special bull which was given to him at the initiation to adulthood.

For my part, I had undertaken the first step, but I missed

the initiation opportunity in late 1986 due to my sickness because I couldn't manage the initiation procedure at the time. But my cousin Magong Dhieu Kiir and two others got their initiation instead. As mentioned, I was very sick but I still held the title of being called a boy, not a man, even though some of my age group had reached that level. Being uninitiated excluded me from many social activities that were undertaken by the initiated men in my area.

The initiation of the boys into adulthood is one of the proudest moments in Dinka society. The Dinka celebrate this stage with happiness and this is compared with the circumcision of Arab boys into adulthood in Muslim communities. The entire community would express joy to welcome the initiated men into their group. Even now I am still longing for my initiation in order to be absorbed into my age generation. Some of these initiated men who used to herd the cattle with me while we were still boys in Ajuba remote area have now acquired the position of Ajuba chieftain while others have obtained various positions of traditional leaders in the community including the position of traditional healers and magicians. The position of Chieftain is the highest position in the community which is occupied by the person who is trusted by the entire community to rule them with the help of the elders. The position of chieftain in my area is more important than the position of the Judge while the magician is adored like the son of God.

Our basic food is the heavy millet porridge eaten with milk or traditional handmade food. Milk itself in various forms is also a primary food in the Dinka areas. The Dinka wear few clothes principally in their own village or when they are going for visit. Dinka old men usually wear no clothes except for the beads around their necks or wrists while Dinka youths used to be absolutely naked in the cattle camp, but in dances or public appearances they would shelter their buttocks with well-trimmed skins of wild bright colored cats. The Dinka women normally wear a couple of sheepskins with one in front and one in the back. These cross around and fall down from the waist parting a gap on either side beginning at the center of the thighs and widen as the skins reach the knees. Both teenage girls and boys would naturally be naked.

The Dinka do not sing at the time of death except in the burial rite of traditional chiefs or spear masters. As soon as a death occurs amongst the family or relatives, a phase of bereavement is observed for one year. Beads and other belongings that allude to cheerfulness are not needed.

The Dinka believe that there is one God who creates heaven and earth. The term that they use for God is Nhialic which means God. They believe that Nhialic is the creator and source of life but is distant from human affairs. The Dinka recognized the existence of the two spheres. The sphere of the Supreme Being (Nhialic) with his home somewhere in the sky where people don't do evil and the sphere of the departed ancestors and relatives (ghosts) whom one can address in times of disasters and tribulations. Nhialic still makes himself known to the people in the form of blessings of rain, as well as health and long life. The Dinka tribe practices various forms of sacrifice, both to bring reconciliation and relationship between one another and the land. Though Nhialic can be petitioned, nobody can really know him because of his greatness. The Dinka contact God or Nhialic through mediators and entities by various rituals. These rituals are administered by diviners and healers. They believe that the spirits of the departed become part of the spiritual sphere of this life. Nhialic can be petitioned to bless friends and curse enemies according to the need of the Dinka. Tradition permits addressing God and the spirits of the departed ancestors and relatives either directly or through a medium in a special offering place (we called it Yiik in Dinka language) situated in every Dinka homestead. In Dinka culture, people call on the power of the spirits to try to heal sicknesses or cast spells on their enemies to make them sick or even kill them. But now most of the Dinka people are being baptized and become true Christians.

The Dinka, like other African people, stress respect both for oneself and others in order to achieve status in the society. The Dinka base their life on values of respect and self-esteem and cherish the notion of stratification in their hierarchy of respect. In Dinka society, the young people always respect and give honour to the elders whether at home or outside it. The Dinka elders are the people who discuss and solve problems in the community meeting.

THE MEANING OF THE COW TO THE DINKA

Cows meant everything and still are very significant in the life of the Dinka tribe everywhere in the Dinka land. Entire communities still lived a very traditional life and cattle were literally central to the whole lives of the Dinka tribe. We used to live in the traditional thatched grass hut built near the byre. The cattle were kept in front of the byre before they were put into the byre at night. I started to look after the cows in the bush when I was about eight years old. This is where I was exposed to the reality that cattle are indeed central to the life of the Dinka people, not only as a supply of food and prosperity but as a root of cheerfulness.

Cows mean everything in the life of the Dinka people; hence they are a key symbol of assets. It is the medium of exchange whether in marriage to pay for the bride or for sacrifices to the spirits or for major occasions and rites. In addition, cows are considered as a form of currency in rural areas of Southern Sudan where money is not visible.

Our dedication to the Dinka life was almost zealous. We would be up before dawn to milk the cows and then collect the cow dung with our bare hands. Taking care of cattle is full-time work for boys in Dinka society. Throughout most of Dinka land, cows were allowed out only to graze. In the evening, the cows would be shut up in a dark cattle byre at night.

Children are also considered as assets among the Dinka people. Young boys before the age of seven began herding calves which require less water. The young boys used to look after the calves which grazed near the villages while the older boys were used to herd cattle in the bush. However, the boys used to be well equipped in order to follow the animals into dangerous unfamiliar areas. In Dinka culture, the job for the boys would be in the morning and in the evening to ensure that the calves did not get out of the byres where they were kept so that they would not go and suckle their mothers before they were milked. The boys got up early in the morning to release the cows for breakfast grazing prior to milking or to tether them outside while they were cleaning the byre. At the time of milking, the boy would allow the calf up to the cow to excite it teats in order to yield milk. Then they would hold the calf back while its mother was being milked, with some milk being left for the calf. Since the cattle byre become messy at night, cleaning the cow dung from the byre was a formidable task for the boys to do.

In the morning, I would assume the task of milking the cows because the Dinka culture does not allow a boy to remain in the hut in the morning or sit by the fire to warm himself. Otherwise they would predict that this boy will come to nothing when he had grown up. He had to go out as soon as dawn broke. It is the work of the boy to go out to the bush to look after the cattle. That is why many boys were sent out to do some work while the girls engaged in the household activities with their mothers or stepmothers. As the cattle boy, I used to carry big pieces of dung with my bare hands in the byre and spread them outside to dry for fuel. My bare feet were often sullied with cow dung and human waste. Therefore, the smoking fire helps the drying process and deodorizes the byre. During the school holidays, I would graze the cattle daily without relief and combine this with fishing in the river.

The cattle served many purposes in Dinka society because their milk and blood are used for food; their urine is used in washing hands, while their hides are used for mattresses. The cows' dung fuels fires from which the ashes are used to keep the cattle clean and free from blood-sucking ticks. In addition, the hides are used as blankets or bedding in the winter season.

The complicated task to memorize as a boy was the practice of coaxing the cows which have lost their calves to accept being milked at some point in the rainy season. You could coax the cows, but the possibility of drinking its urine was also frequent because when you coaxed the cows, they can urinate without warning and the whole urine could end up in your hungry mouth. It is one of the works that I hated, but being a Dinka boy I had no choice but to do the job as required. The cows were milked once in the morning and once in the evening. We used to drink cow urine mixed with milk but not the cow urine alone except at the time of coaxing when you could sip the cow urine by mistake. Usually I used to herd the cattle in the bush through rain or shine.

The Dinka valued their cattle as a source of life-giving liquid during the famine. Before the war displaced me from my village in Southern Sudan, our main foods were maize, sorghum and other crops that were produced in our field. We would drink fresh milk as well as sour milk. We would also eat cattle blood for the reason that we would bleed the cattle and capture the spilled blood into the gourds for drinking to sustain life. Sometime we would eat solid food and used to wait until it was out of our system to drink milk again. Mixing the two was viewed to be very bad for the cattle. We would also eat veal when the cows had produced calves. Being the cattle boy, I used to spread my body with cows ghee which I detested very much for the reason that it smelled foul to me. But it seemed to me that the foul-smelling products of the cows, including its dung, were treated like perfumes by the rural people at the time. I understood at an early age that you could love animals and still eat them. My parents were cattle owners and simple farmers because their social aspect of living was dependent upon animals and crop production. In the Dinka language, cows get their names according to the color of the animal and other descriptive attributes. A Dinka boy is initiated into cattle life thus they are the ones who herd and milk the cows, while Dinka men only birth calves and dance for the best bull, not cows or oxen, except in the burial rite of the traditional chiefs or spear masters.

It was in the grazing fields that I learned how to rob the wild honey from the bees to drink with other boys in the bush. I would hunt rats with these boys and we would burn the few rats that we were able to kill and eat them heartily in the bush. I still remember the time when I hastily caught the tail of a live rat in the hole and pulled it out. I thought it was not harmful but soon after I pulled it out, the rat bit my finger. In addition, I would spend some time in the hedge place to battle with other boys during the day. In the evenings, I would share the meal calmly with the same boys that we were combating previously as if nothing has happened during the day. In my culture, a boy who remained at home beside his mother was called ahotic in Dinka language. I also learned stick fighting which is an essential part of the life of any Dinka boy before his initiation into adulthood in the Dinka society. In Dinka traditions, the boys would start to practice stick fighting and spear dueling with great dexterity from their youth. After that, I would carry the traditional walking sticks as well as spears and clubs as a means of safety at all times in our village. One day, I pricked myself with my herding stick in my right shin, which led to infection but eventually it healed.

Spiritually, the Dinka blessed their oxen and then slaughtered them to their family spirits in exchange for rain and the health of the entire community. The animals were blessed with tribal prayers by the conjurers and then slaughtered. Cattle have a religious significance and they are the first choice as the animal of sacrifice though sheep may be sacrificed as a substitute on occasion. The meat of the cows were rarely taken for food but was used during ceremonies and times of famines. The oxen would only be killed for big ceremonies to praise the ancestors and family spirits by the master of spears in the area. Sacrifices were made to family spirits (Yath) since Nhialic (God) is too distant for direct contact with humans. The bulls and oxen as well as cow milk were offered as sacrifices to the family spirits. The family and general social relations are primary values in Dinka religious thought. In Dinka traditional beliefs, sacrifice is a necessary part of devotion and without shedding of blood there is no significant worship. There were three traditional gods to be worshipped in my society before Christianity came: they were the clan spirits, section spirits and family spirits. The Kiir Arieu family used to pray to our own family spirit known as Michar

Lual Kiir. My mother is still committed to the worship of our family spirits and sticks to her traditional beliefs at the moment because she is an animist.

Before Christianity, the major influence formerly was exercised by chiefs of the fishing spears or spear masters. These elite groups provided health through mystical power. Their role has been eradicated due to changes brought about by western missionaries and the modern world. The Dinka society was egalitarian with no class system. All people, wealthy or poor, were expected to contribute to the common good. The primary art forms were poetry and songs. The Dinka modeled clay pots with decorations. The Dinka influenced the shape of their oxen's horns by carving the tips of their horns in a desired way before the horns mature. There were certain types of songs for different types of activities of life like festive occasions and preparation for war as well as burial rites. History and social identity were taught and preserved through songs. The Dinka frequently sang the praise songs to their ancestors and to the living. In Dinka Society, the songs were even used ritually in competition to resolve a quarrel in a legal sense.

CHRISTIANITY AND CUSTOMARY FAITHFULNESS

Before I become a Christian, I was afraid of Church, both the building and the meaning of it, without knowing it because I grew up in a home with traditional influences and morals. Our family and relatives were deeply involved in traditional gods practice and the ritual traditional occasions were as much a part of our lives as breathing was. My mother was and is still animist who regularly offered up animal sacrifices to the spirits of the dead. We never went to Church nor bothered to hear anything about Jesus Christ. In addition, being a born-again Christian in the Dinka society during those days was a taboo. If you converted your relatives would angrily disown you and say that vengeful spirits would soon kill you for ignoring the traditional beliefs of your ancestors. As a youth, I was very interested in the matters of the traditional gods and was involved with the activities of our local magicians. I would sit near the magicians as they would worship the traditional gods. The magicians would spread out the meats as ritual offerings to the family spirits in our area and I would collect the scattered meats on the ground with other children in the area. Traditional ceremonies were held in which all of my ancestors were evoked as our relatives would communicate to our ancestors who would pass the message on to God. My late maternal grandmother used to say that our ancestors were nearest to God and we have lived with them. It is the tradition of our culture and my mother is still sticking to it.

I had always heard the name Jesus Christ and I didn't know who he was or what he did, but the idea of going into a Church building frightened me. I thought that if I stepped into a Church building I would burst into flames. As one of the animist child, I used to collect the meat thrown down by the local traditional healers as a traditional gift to family spirits in my area with other children of my age. When my friend invited me to attend a Church service at the Christmas party, it must have been the hand of God that led me to go with them because there was no way I would set foot in a church building. After I went to the Church then I learned who God is. However, I mustered up courage and spoke to my mother about my desire to be baptized. She was happy with my decision because my mother was not a prisoner of religious belief. With the support of Apiu Michar and my fellow Christians in Ajuba area, I was baptized in January 1981 by the late Right Reverend Peter Monywac Yol, Vice-Moderator of the Presbyterian Church of the Sudan. How cheerful I was to have my late maternal aunt Akon Ayuel Koryom and my elder sister Areng Chol Lual attends my baptism. After my baptism, Apiu Michar, wife of my late half brother Kon Mamor Lual took me under her wing and taught me to grow to be a successful Christian. I remain greatly indebted to her for her example and caring help. Furthermore, the Christian lesson Mrs. Apiu Michar taught me made it possible for me to love my enemies and forgive them completely.

Chapter 3

FORGIVING MY ABUSIVE RELATIVE

I had big relatives in which there was one abusive individual named Dol Kiir Lual and his friend Mirial Chan Bayek. I was aware of him and got to know about his cruelty when I was as young as six years old. As a child, I grew up in a horrible situation. My callous brother Dol Kiir Lual was an abusive man both verbally and physically. He nearly killed my mother when I was six year old. He would beat me up all the time and beat my mother often. He would also beat my older sister Areng Chol Lual like a donkey. Therefore, fear was a part of my life and it upset me extremely to see my mother suffer. For these reasons, I truly hated what our lives were and I went all the way through life angry with God about why he had killed my own father and left us in the hands of an abusive half brother. When I was in my early teens, I developed a hatred toward my abusive brother Dol Kiir Lual to the point where I was yearning to take revenge against him when I become an adult due to his mistreatment toward my widowed mother, my sister Areng and me. Whether it was rain or shine, I would go to the bush to herd the cattle after milking and I did what my abusive half brother Dol Kiir Lual told me to do. We served him like slaves from morning to night time. I was up in the early morning to milk the cows and my mother would sweep the compound, fetching fire wood and foodstuffs from the farm, as well as fetching water from the stream. The abuse that I suffered at the hands of my brother Dol Kiir Lual as well as my route as a teenager has left its blot on my character. I did not have a single minute to myself to relax because I was a restless child. But all these things did not lead me to denounce my relatives for their failure to criticize my abusive half brother Dol Kiir Lual. In the evening, I would milk the cows again and put them in the byre. In addition, I would go out fishing in the river or hunting in the nearby forest with the family dogs. I was not a naughty child even when my heartless half brother Dol

Kiir Lual would provoke me. This remained precise through my teen years as well. I was an unexciting child, at least in my own eyes. As a teen, I was forced to work with my mother after school in the farm while the other children in the neighbourhood were free to pursue their own interests. We worked in mud so thick that it made our feet as heavy as elephant feet. On weekends, we went to the field to reap the crops. We would start our work at daybreak and finish after dusk, aching and hungry from the work of making food. My half brother Dol Kiir Lual would get drunk before dinner each evening and spend the rest of the night quarrelling with my mother, even after I went to sleep. Listening to his raised voice would fill me with annoyance to my abusive half brother Dol Kiir Lual for causing the dilemma.

To make the situation even more complicated, my elder sister Areng Chol Lual have been assigned by my spiteful half brother Dol Kiir Lual to a husband she did not want to marry. The man who was assigned to marry my sister was called Majok who was later caught by lawless Nuer militants in Ajuba area and killed along with others in Anakdiar village. My sister refused openly that she would not accept this marriage, despite the countless consequences she would face from her refusal. Beyond a doubt, we all paid a heavy price for her refusal. We have gone through horrible mistreatments and so on. I will never forget the day my mother was attacked as a result of this issue. The refusal of my sister Areng Chol Lual to marry the above-mentioned man brought untold misery to my mother who was accused of siding with her daughter by my rude half brother Dol Kiir Lual and his friend Mirial Chan Bayek. The two men vowed to even kill my mother for failing to convince her daughter to be marry by the man because they had taken his cows as a bride price secretly in advance. My abusive half brother Dol Kiir Lual ordered his friend Mr. Mirial Chan Bayak to attack my mother by hitting her head with the fighting stick with the intention of killing her which he attempted. I will never forget the evening that Mirial Chan Bayek attacked my mother and almost broke her right arm. The poor man has been led like a blind man by my half brother Dol Kiir Lual ever since. I don't know where the two illiterate men would have ended up at the time of my adulthood, if their attempts to kill my mother had been successful. As the situation became tense, my mother appealed many times in tears to my sister Areng to marry the man she was engaged to. Although that made my sister feel awful, she did not change her mind to be married to the man in question. After my half brother Dol Kiir Lual failed to convince my sister Areng, he then became enraged. After all the efforts have failed, however, he set on fire the barn that held sorghum and claimed that his crops could not be eaten by the dogs, by which he meant my mother and her children, including myself. The detestation that I felt for my pitiless half brother Dol Kiir Lual was so intense that I frequently thought of murdering him, even though I knew I could never fulfill such an act. In addition, being raised in a home where there was only one parent often caused me to be frustrated and resentful of my missing father, coupled with being treated as an outcast for most of my childhood. I was the wretched child who had experienced hardship very, very much.

My half brother Dol Kiir Lual was not only cruel as mentioned above, he was corrupt. He had eaten away our belongings through his unjust actions toward us. But when I became a Christian, I forgave my scoundrel half brother Dol Kiir Lual for the horrible things he had done toward us, something I thought I would never be able to do. I had also forgiven his faithful friend Mirial Chan Bayek for what he had done to my mother. I was able to forgive my half brother Dol Kiir Lual even though he is still dishonest to our family and relatives in Sudan at the moment. Furthermore, Mirial Chan Bayek had three daughters of his own without a single son in his name that he could use as shield in case of future retribution. When I met him in Baliet town after I had visited the area in 2001 with my mother, he almost fainted with the awful memory as he saw me with my mother, whom he had attempted to kill. The looks of the frail old man needed no further translations of sorrow for his past involvement in abusing my mother. As the dreadful memory and reminiscence clicked in my mind, I almost overlooked him several times before we were able to swap a few words and share some rare laughs. After that, we sat down together for the first time and managed to share the food grudgingly, like political enemies. During those periods, we faced many tests and difficulties ranging from financial problems to physical sickness.

My mother has been the cornerstone on which I have found the strength to carry on. Any widowed mother knows how difficult it is to make ends meet by working as a cultivator and having the time to care for her children at the end of the day.

PRIMARY SCHOOLING IN AJUBA REMOTE AREA

I started my schooling at the age of about nine in Riangnom Primary school and I completed grade three before the civil war had closed most of the schools in Southern Sudan. In the beginning, I hated the school and felt that there were more exciting things to do than stare at a blackboard. As I got a little older I was sent to school by myself, I often sneaked away to a local sorghum field to chew the cane and spit out all the way with my cousin Magong Dhieu Kiir during the time my mother thought I was spending in school. It was the insistence of my half brother Dhieu Kiir Lual that obligated me to continue my studies and finally make my progress in school. But I never truly liked school and I was scared of the teachers. In addition, I was uninterested in the school lessons held in the open air because I had come from a family who could neither read nor write with any degree of proficiency. But my half brother Dhieu Kiir Lual, who was the senior official in the government of Upper Nile State, made various material sacrifices for me, making it possible for me to have an education and I began to enjoy school more. Honestly, I would like to salute my dear brother Dhieu Kiir Lual for his effort to put me through school and I credit him for persuading me to pursue my education. On the other hand, my brother Dhieu Kiir Lual was more committed for those "who scratch not their hearts but their clothes." My brother Dhieu Kiir Lual was the determining influence on me throughout my childhood. I loved him very much and I believe once I look back that he must have singled me out amongst my siblings for particular interest. It was he who inspired me to have an education which I did on his own request despite the resistance from my mother and my maternal grandmother who were against the so-called school. In fact, he was open-minded enough to know that I should go to school. However, he moved me from Wune Kuanynok village where I used to stay with my late maternal grandmother Arop Monyjok Reth, fifteen miles away from the school, to Wune Adol village, ten miles nearer the school so that I would have less distance to walk. So from about the age of nine I would walk ten miles to Riangnom primary school in Ajuba district through a grassy and muddy road full of snakes and scorpions. The snakes and scorpions used to nibble people constantly while they walked into the water. It was not relaxing because I had to go to school through the rain and walking barefoot, something that disturbed my children as I told them about my early life. There were neither school buses nor transport of any kind to take the students to the school. I would leave home for school in the morning, hungry for knowledge and later come back home, hungry for food because there was no lunch program in the school. For this reason, I ate my food once a day in the evening after I returned home from school. There was no electricity in the area and I used to read my books sometimes by the light of the moon. This practice helped me a lot during my ups and downs in various refugee camps before I came to Canada.

Baliet County is a swamp land where the snakes and scorpions are often in sight. Initially, most school buildings were of mud walls. All the rooms were overcrowded so the rest of students were taught under the trees, including myself, before I was transferred to a single mud hut with a grass-thatched roof for forty five pupils that had to be evacuated when it rained. In school, the teachers taught us the alphabet and basic counting. We did not have any exercise books to write in and there were only two copies of the alphabet books from which we would copy the alphabet, writing it in the sand with our forefingers. We would normally sit on the dusty floor because there were no school benches during those days in my village school.

There I studied Arabic along with other subjects. When I turned age fifteen, I began to think seriously about how to continue my education. My mother, however, did not like this idea of the so-called school and my maternal grandmother Arop Monyjok Reth was strongly opposed to the so-called school for cultural reasons. Dinka boys who used to go to school were viewed as cowards and thieves by the entire community because there were misunderstandings about the school by the villagers in those days. The parents thought that their children are going to school to be taught to be thieves by the teachers instead of becoming the doctors or lawyers, etc. That is why most of the Dinka children were resentful toward the formal education for mainly cultural reasons.

In spite of the resistance from my mother and my maternal grandmother, my brother Dhieu Kiir urged them to let me go to school because my brother Dhieu Kiir Lual hoped that my education would lead to good employment and economic help for the entire families of Lual Kiir Arieu in the future. My brother Dhieu Kiir Lual is a man full of truth and he was the person who had inspired me to have an education even though my mother was strongly opposed on cultural grounds. As I look back, it seemed to me that my brother Dhieu Kiir Lual had provided me with the rare chance of education which I could not have had without his pressure. I still regard him like my second father for the golden chance that he provided me to have an education and made sure that I met his expectations. I thought he must have known this and made it as his main concern to inspire me to meet his wishes which I did so for his sake.

Since the civil war broke out in 1983, I could not to go school for three years. In early 1984, many areas were heavily militarized by the Sudan Armed Forces and its allies of militias. As a result, these areas were viewed as military targets by the Sudan People Liberation Army (SPLA) and local communities were considered as security threats by Sudan Armed Forces based in the area. As such, it was the ground for heavy fighting between the Sudan Armed Forces and the SPLA forces;

thus it was not possible for us to have classes. Before the school was closed permanently, we were not allowed to stay on school grounds after school activities because of the insecurity in the area.

My mother was opposed to my education for traditions reasons; thus she was put under a great deal of pressure by my brother Dhieu Kiir Lual who was in desperate need of my education. He wanted me to learn in order to become a responsible individual as I grew up and make contributions to society. He would tell me these words: Train a child in the way he should go and then when he is old, he will not turn away from it, as declared in Proverbs 22:6. This scripture was the word from my brother Dhieu Kiir Lual for me to follow and accomplish.

On an educational level amongst my family, I was the first person who had access to education. My younger brother Dhot followed suit, but my mother and my two surviving sisters are illiterate. They cannot read and write in Dinka, let alone Arabic. Although my mother is illiterate, she was the person who raised me and taught me to serve others and honour God or Nhialic, as she called God.

Many of the things I learned early on as a child from my mother were to practice patience which has helped me throughout many ups and downs in my adult life. I never thought much about any of these things until the day I ran out of funds in Khartoum during the process of my immigration to Egypt in 2002. Were it not for the lessons that I have learned from my mother, I might never think about helping other deprived people at the moment. But for me, the suffering and anxiety that I have endured since my early childhood have helped me later in life. It gave me the strength and taught me values like hard work. However, education in my society was an informal affair. Thus most children were used to spending some time engaged in non-school activities like herding cattle or milking cows. Apart from daily training for the discipline of work, the mind was trained through story telling, including traditional songs. At night, people would have a game after eating or drinking sour milk from the gourd. Personally, school was not in my mind nor was it on my list of things to achieve in life. My desire was to follow in the footsteps of my late father Chol Lual Kiir as a cattle keeper and a dancer with the girls in the Ajuba area, as well as having jokes with the girls as was customary in the Dinka culture before marriage.

A BRIEF HISTORY OF SUDAN

Sudan is the largest country in Africa. It occupies an area of almost one million square miles. This is equal to the United Kingdom, France, Italy and all the Scandinavian countries combined. Sudan borders Egypt in the north, Libya in the northwest, Chad and Central African Republic in the west, Eritrea and Ethiopia in the east, the Democratic Republic of Congo in the southeast, Uganda and Kenya in the south and southeast correspondingly. Sudan is broadly divided into two regions: North and South. The north is largely Muslim and Arab in both speech and culture. On the other hand, populations of native peoples such as the people of the Nuba Mountains and the Beja still preserve their long-established cultures and habits of life, surviving Islamic cultural offensive and oppression for centuries. The South, in contrast is Christian and animist. The population of Sudan is estimated at about forty five million people. Muslims compose of seventy per cent of the population while Christians and animists make up thirty per cent of the population. In total, there are sixty four significant tribes in Southern Sudan that speak different languages and dialects. Population growth is 2.2% per annum with a life expectancy of 54 years for male and 58 years for female. According to 2008 statistics, the child mortality rate is 100 per 1000 live births in Southern Sudan.

Sudan became an independent state on January 1, 1956 after over 60 years of Anglo- Egyptian rule. Even before independence, in 1955 the South mutinied against the North. This was the start of the first civil war called Anya-Nya (poisonous snakes.) This term has come to stand for resistance against the North. During this conflict, it is estimated that two million people lost their lives and another million people became refugees in neighboring countries. After 17 years of fighting, President Jaffer Numeiri realized that the conflict must be solved political-ly. In 1972 consultations were convened between the Southern Sudan Liberation Movement (SSLM) and the military regime of Jaffer Numeiri in Addis Ababa in Ethiopia. An accord was signed at this time that granted the South autonomy under a united Sudan. Ten years of relative peace followed, however, in time, the accord became destabilized and mutilated by north-ern politicians. President Jaffer Numeiri publicly decreed the abrogation of the 1972 Addis Ababa accord and declared Sharia (Islamic) law throughout the entire nation.

Chagai Chol Lual

Chapter 4

BACKGROUND ABOUT THE CIVIL WAR IN SUDAN

On 16 May 1983, Southerners formed the Sudan People Liberation Movement and Sudan People Liberation Army (SPLM/SPLA) headed by Dr. John Garang Mabior. The objective of the SPLM/SPLA was to fight for democratic participation, freedom and equality for all citizens regardless of race, gender or religion beliefs. The intention of the Sudan People Liberation Movement and Sudan People Liberation Army (SPLM/A) was to fight against the former president, Jaffer Numeir. The challenge presented to the government by the SPLM/SPLA sent shock waves to Khartoum regime, leading to two military coups in 1985 and 1989. On June 30, 1989, President Omer Beshir came to power by coup and claimed a jihad (Islamic Holy war) against the South. Shortly after the formation of the SPLM/SPLA, the Khartoum regime mobilized mainly Arab militias who are currently accused of atrocities in Darfur to kill the Southerners in Southern Sudan. The Arab militias that were deployed in Southern Sudan were spearheaded by cannon fodder expecting to be martyrs who they mostly became. This made it clear that Islam is a well known religion that promotes the killing of non-Muslims as the path to heaven. In addition, the Sudan Armed Forces and its friendly militias that were deployed in Southern Sudan were mistreating the civilian population and tortures were common. The Arabs had been calling for Muslims to rally around Holy war in northern Sudan against the infidels in Southern Sudan. In addition, the Khartoum regime recklessly endangered civilians by using excessive force, including air strikes in residential areas and the killing of innocent civilians. Above all, the Khartoum regime armed and sponsored southern militias in Southern Sudan in particular to continue their battle with the SPLA forces and terrorized the civilians in their villages. Most of those casualties were caused by the Sudan Armed Forces who seemed to have no regard for civilian life. On the other hand, the Nuer prophet Wud Nyang Gatkek too called for Holy war against the Dinka and ethnic cleansing. The government troops and ethnic militias burned huts and set fire to stores of grain that held supplies of sorghum and maize in the entire area of Dinka Ngok land. The Khartoum regime used to sponsor the ethnic militias in Southern Sudan to divide Southerners against each others with the goal of abating the SPLM/A movement.

On the 9th of January in 2005, a peace agreement was signed by all parties, including the Government of Sudan and Sudan People Liberation Movement (SPLM), under the presence of IGAD, witnessed by international observers in Nairobi in Kenya. Over the past 22 years, over two million lives have been claimed in the conflict and over twice this amount of people have become displaced. After the peace agreement was signed, the leader of the SPLM, Dr. John Garang Mabior, was named First Vice-President and President of the Government of Southern Sudan on July 9th, 2005. He was killed three weeks later in a mysterious plane crash while returning from neighbouring Uganda on 30 July, 2005. Dr. John Garang Mabior was the second Sudanese First Vice President and the fourth Sudanese politician to die in a plane crash in Sudan. Moreover, the First Vice-President Al Zubeir Mohamed Salih was killed in the plane crash in 1998 while the State Minister of Defence Ibrahim Shams Al din was killed in a plane crash in 2001. The chief Negotiator, Mr. Abu Gisseisa, died in a plane crash in 1993 along with the Governor of Upper Nile State, Mr. Paul Reth Kuany. The late hero Dr. John Garang Mabior embodied the future of a country with hopes of bringing change to a nation where the people of Southern Sudan were treated as third class citizens in their own country, where Muslim men were regarded as first class citizens and Muslim women as second class citizens since the independence from Britain in 1956. After the mysterious death of Dr. John Garang Mabior, he was succeeded by Lieutenant General Salva Kiir Mayardit as First Vice President of the Republic of Sudan and President of the Government of Southern Sudan.

CIVIL WAR BROUGHT HUMAN SUFFERINGS

Civil war disrupted my peaceful childhood as well as that of my own generation who were raised during this enduring war in Southern Sudan. Dodging the incoming bullets, suffering hunger, being displaced and sleeping in the cold were part of my life. I often crawled courageously into the bush to hide from the approaching government soldiers. I slept in the cold because of the persistent fleeing from incoming government soldiers who used to attack civilian targets. The damage from the war took many worse forms than just shelling holes in Southern Sudan. I suffered terrible nightmares and ravages to my stomach after becoming accustomed to eating only one meal per day in the Refugee Camp. My stomach became used to eating only one meal a day and I continue to follow this practice today. Before the war, every family had the right to eat and drink as they could afford but the war limited the freedom of eating and drinking. I grew up in the refugee camp after I fled the war zone. My life was a life of struggle. In reality, the war itself stole my genera-tion in Southern Sudan. War was all we have known for a long time instead of peace and stability. We have known panic and uncertainty as we have never lived normal lives nor have we enjoyed sovereignty and freedom like other human beings on the globe. In addition, the human loss that I have experienced during the war in Southern Sudan was great. I lost my mater-nal uncle Abiel Ayuel Koryom in 1989 when he was killed by a land mine in Baliet area. I also lost Monyjur Mayiik Agau bet-ter known as Monyjur Nyanayul Lual Kiir who was killed in Toriet in Southern Sudan in 1989. Moreover, I lost a number of close friends, not to mention neigbours and acquaintances. Some families in Southern Sudan have been completely wiped out in the war that claimed the lives of two million Sudanese people and displaced more than five million people in Southern Sudan, alone, making it one of the worst disasters in history.

FLEEING THE MILITANTS RAID IN RUANYRUANY

In 1984 soon after the formation of the SPLM/A, the Khartoum regime ordered the mass killing of the Dinka people in Southern Sudan. All the villages of the Dinka tribe were attacked and burned to the ground. The Khartoum regime would encourage the Nuer militias to attack the SPLA and terrorize villagers in Southern Sudan, especially in the Dinka areas. The Nuer ethnic militias would raid the Dinka cattle and burn their villages to the ground. In October 1985, the Nuer militants, sponsored by the Sudanese government, attacked the village of Ruanyruany in Ajuba area. This attack claimed the life of Mijok Lim and displaced many people in the area while countless cows were looted. During this attack, I ran into the grassland which turned out to be a worse enemy than the heartless Nuer Militants. Walking in the grassland on foot with the cattle was so complicated that if the Nuer militiamen had had the audacity to track me, I would have been a simple target with the cattle that were mooing all the way. In fact, the militia had given up the chase. I shall never forget those two nights that I spent in the grassland with the cattle. The odds were stacked against me because I was moving with the cattle through the wide grassland leaving a clear pathway which any vengeful Nuer militants could have followed. I wandered alone in the bush with my cattle because a number of the men whom I asked to go with me in Ruanyruany were just selfish men, to say the least, and had already refused to let my cows be mixed with their cows due to the tick-born diseases that my cows had. Even though these merciless Ajuba men in Ruanyruany were well aware of my young age to be wandering alone, they did not have enough compassion to welcome me with my cattle into their group. Instead, I wandered alone in the bush where I spent two sleepless nights before I reached Wuol Miyom Wuor village with the cattle. Stumbling through the thick grass, I got lost and nearly starved. Imagine the feelings of my anxious mother when she saw me leave on my own, in spite of my boyhood. This was the first time I had been away from home, basically on my own and I enjoyed it. But who knew what hungry wild animals might have eaten me in the bush, I thought to myself as I followed the cows deeper into the mosquito-infested jungle. Those two nights were the most sleepless nights I ever had in my life because the night was so cold and I was barefoot and wore no clothes, not even the little piece of cloth to cover my freezing buttocks. As it began to get dark, I got worried. My mother feared that I might have been eaten by the wild animals in the bush. She silently prayed that the spirits of my departed relatives would guard me throughout my journey. But to my own joy, the animals were also terrified by the gunfire in the bush and were running for their own safety, except for the lion that was lying closely in the tall grass where I was sitting. Being in the darkest night, I didn't know that I might have been sitting near the lion in the tall grass, however, it was my aggressive bull that went around provoking the lion. When the lion roared, my heart felt like it had been ripped from my chest and I almost dead of fear in the bush alone. Thank God that the lion did not eat me because it was running from the gunshot, like me. So I braved the long night near the lion until the lion moved away, following the sunrise in the next morning. Following the second night, I thought I would be free to spend the night without worry but such was not the case. In the bush along the way, I tried to sleep on the layers of the grass surrounded by my cattle. This time the hyenas surrounded me in the distance, their roars filling the darkness. After another sleepless night, I found out that they were not paying attention to me but to the deer that had been dumped close by. It took me two days of walking and two sleepless nights before I arrived in Wuol village with the cows and I dozed whenever I had to sit. But the days before my arrival at Wuol village were the worst because I hadn't eaten anything for two days in the bush. I was really suffering from cold and was nearly starving. By the time I arrived in Wuol village, I was really tired and weak from hunger, and I was looking forward to getting rest. I was warmly received by Mr. Machol Chan Bayek with his late wife Nyariak Miyom Wuor. After that, I told Machol that I was ready to sleep but I needed something to eat. His late wife Nyariak Miyom Wuor rushed up in unbelievable time and brought me a traditional dish almost overflowing with food to warm my mouth. As I grabbed the traditional spoon to eat, my boring emaciated eyes somehow shined as I swallowed the first little bite of food. It was the first food I had eaten for three days and I ate it speedily like a soldier. After I helped myself with the hot meal, then I tried to rest in the grass thatched hut that Machol had given me to sleep in. Later, Machol sheltered my cattle in his cow byre in the evening. Five hours before sunset, my feet ached and were swollen; hence the pains did not grant me an opportunity to doze. In the evening, the lightly thatched grass hut that Machol had given me to sleep in was full of holes in the roof. I was bare-foot and naked in the cold winter. By midnight, the most vicious cold I have ever experienced struck me with a vengeance and I began to cough up some blood.

Chapter 5

BATTLING TO SURVIVE DURING MY ILLNESS

I soon settled in Wuol Miyom Wuor village to enjoy my cattle herding activity, but this was not to last. After two days, I got very sick probably due to the mosquito bites from the bush. I had to be taken to my mother in Wune Kuanyok village by Machol Chan Bayek and his friend. My mother Nyanbuny was living in Wune Kuanyok village with my siblings and my late maternal grandmother Arop Monyjok Reth. Upon our arrival in Wune Kuanyok, Machol Chan Bayek asked my younger sister Nyanyiik if my mother was at home. Abruptly, my sister Nyanyiik, shouted loudly in Dinka language, "Mama, Mama", meaning "my mother, my mother, there are two men and a sick boy at the door." My sister Nyanyiik showed no sign of recognizing me as she ran into the house to inform my mother. When my mother saw me, she was so embarrassed with tears streaming down in her face. Seeing my concerned mother crying like a baby made me feel bad and I soon started to cry which increased her shock. My mother would keep praying to Nhialic about my recovery.

My late maternal grandmother Arop Monyjok Reth was not at home during the time of my arrival. She was still working in her field so she did not hear of my illness or my whereabouts with the cattle. Shortly after her arrival from work, she recognized me because I was lying helpless on the mat, too weak to swat away the flies that swirled around my face in our small thatched grass hut. As soon as my dear maternal grandmother Arop saw me in such a state, she shouted in Dinka language and wearily threw up her hands asking Nhialic for my recovery. She vowed to give up her own life for my sake asking God or Nhialic in Dinka language to take her own life if needed for my recovery because she deemed her own death not too big for her for my survival. My maternal grandmother Arop Monyjok Reth prayed to the family spirits and ancestors about my recovery. She sang the traditional songs by calling on our ancestral spirits for my healing. I dealt with my occasional bouts of malaria and my relatives coped with some worries caused by my illness.

Shortly, the word of my sickness spread like wildfire to my relatives and neighbors. Along with my close relatives who came to see me first was my late maternal aunt Akon Ayuel Koryom. I will never forget my dear aunt arriving and almost collapsing to the ground as she stepped into the house and saw me because I was lying shakily on the mat. After a few seconds my late maternal aunt broke into tears and cried appallingly. She keenly asked God or Nhialic for my healing saying, "God, forgive us, this one son of my sister whom we are placing our hope on." There were no telephone lines in those days so the news were passed by word of mouth.

Finally, my aged half brother, the late Ayiei Kiir Deng, a spiritually powerful man among our relatives woke up and grabbed the sacred spear of our family spirits Michar Lual Kiir, plus his adet, and summoned our ancestors and family spirits to try to cure my illness. (Adet is a type of plant that grows in Southern Sudan and is used as a light shield by Dinka men for protection during stick fighting. It is also used as container to keep the tobacco and money, as well as being used as a pillow.) He prayed the rest of the night for my healing, begging God or Nhialic in Dinka language as well as the family spirits and the ancestors to take him if required for my recovery. My half brother Ayiei Kiir, though he was strong of spirit, tried unsuccessfully to hold back his tears as he prayed about my recovery. I supposed that he was speaking directly with God, demanding desperately for my healing from the illness.

After ten months indoors, I was able to recover gradually and it took me another three more months to learn to walk again like a normal human being. My mother took me to a number of so-called traditional healers in our area but all in vain, because there was neither a clinic nor a single doctor in Ajuba area in those days to attend the patient. Seeing a doctor in a larger centre like Malakal was out of the question, because of the long distance. There were no doctors or nurses and those who were sick used to seek out traditional healers for their own cures when they were sick. I was taken to the healers who happened to tell my mother that the cause of my illness lay with my family spirits. If you were sick, during those days in the Ajuba rural area, then you might need eight strong men to carry you about thirty miles to the hospital in Malakal. Otherwise it is your problem with your own God and that is why most of the villagers were heavily relying on local healers and traditional magicians who usually charged them with sheep or goats. Local healers were used to behead the cocks for the traditional healing to ask their ancestors and family spirits for the healing of their patients. During those days, many people in Southern Sudan turned to traditional healers to address their problems rather than the conventional western health system. My mother would check me always to make sure that I was still breathing. Constantly, my late maternal grandmother would pray beside my sleeping mat before she went to her field to cultivate. My mother vowed that she would take her own life as soon as I died so that she might be buried together with me on the same day. She prayed to Nhialic always for my recovery by saying: Nhialic de kuarkuo pale yen menh tong diene" which means "God of our ancestors, forgive me this only son of mine and save his life."

As my legs grew weaker, falling down became a common problem. Sometimes I could walk with the help of a stick or crawl like a child, rather than stand up by myself. As a result, I lost the ability to walk on my own and relied on others to help me walk. Eventually, I could not walk alone without any help. As I have become helpless, my mother was the constant cheerful escort and sources of support during my illness, though my relatives were most generous in their support. After I became gravely ill, my relatives held my hands to help me walk. Some even came over to our house to help take care of me. I dealt with the disappointment caused by my illness, but the most difficult part was the chronic pain that I have to endure without any medication.

THE DAWDLING ROAD TO THE RECUPERATION

As my health was declining, I would fall down like a tree and those around me would be horrified and hurry to help. But I would often make a funny story to shatter the anxiety of my mother and relatives. One day I was walking around the house with my mother and I suddenly fell backward and hit my head badly. When my mother saw me on the ground, her eyes filled with tears before she grabbed me by the hands. She asked me in palpable shock if I was all right and I told her calmly that I was actually fine to decrease her tears. To be honest, I was in terrible pain, yet I didn't want my mother to worry about my health condition. Stunned by the fall, I had a dreadful ache which in turn made my body painful for days. Once I tried another attempt to walk around in the corn field near our house to see whether I would walk again like normal human being. The wind nearly swept me off my feet and I resolved to crawl like a baby to avoid falling down. Once more, I tried another attempt to stand up but my legs were wobbly and I fell right back down. I tried to walk around our house and I stumbled, but I immediately shouted to my mother that I was fine. Struggling to walk again like a normal human being was a slow process before I was able to walk again without the help of a stick. But I still used a walking stick and my walking stick was now there beside me just in case. Eventually, I was walking on my own and I almost fell down again but soon I dropped to my knees and crawled like infant. After many struggles, I could leave my walking stick behind and walk like a normal human being.

ESCAPING FROM THE CIVIL WAR TO ETHIOPIA

I fled my rich farming area in Ajuba district with my cousins to escape the attack of government troops on my village during the Sudanese civil war in 1987. We were accompanied by Nyanber Monyluak Ayuel, the fourth wife of my half brother Dhieu Kiir Lual as our guardian. We braved the desert and attacks by militiamen and Sudan Armed Forces on our way to Ethiopia where we trekked across a thousand miles of wind-swept desert on foot at night, guided by moonlight and then rested during the day. We survived the one-thousand mile trek from my village in Southern Sudan to the refugee camp in Ethiopia. On our way to Ethiopia, we would often ask some Nuer people if Kuanylou village was still far or nearer to reach it. We were not aware of the differing perceptions of distance perceptions that the Nuer people had. The Nuer, mostly women, seemed to us that they were lying by saying "Kuanylou ci thiak elong" in Nuer language, meaning that Kuanylou is near enough to reach it today. I eventually learned that if the Nuer people, especially women, said that the village is just nearest, it usually means that it was still too far to reach it soon. The Nuer people would not tell you the truth about how long it would take you to reach the village which you were asking for. Instead, they would simply tell you that the village in front of you is nearer. But in reality the village of Kuanylou that we were asking about took us five days to reach. Yet the Nuer still insisted that it would take us about an hour to reach it. From a thirteen-year-old's perspective I concluded that the Nuer, especially women, were common liars, more than other ethnic groups I had ever met in Southern Sudan. There was a saying that the Nuer people would lie rather than tell the truth, something the Dinka people would not practiced. The Dinka people would not trick somebody, especially a passerby, when the distance from one village to another village is really far, but the Nuer did so to send you away from their village to the desert instead of hanging around in their village.

When I brought up this lying topic to the attention of my classmates from Nuer tribe who were in the school with me in the Refugee Camp in Ethiopia, the Nuer boys simply told me that they were taught to lie to those outside their own tribe, like Dinka people, whom they treated as their common enemy than Arabs. They assured me that the lies brought them close to those who shared their perception in confrontations against their common enemy. The Nuer boys gave me a major headache when they had explained this topic to me, including sending the hungry Dinka to the desert where they could possibly starve or die of thirst. But who really cares while it was the war time where everyone has been forced to flee their ancestor lands? Later on I realized that perhaps the Nuer women told us the next village was so close in order to give us hope, not to give up if we learned that the journey was going to be so long.

We walked along dirt roads with bare feet and deep hearts. As desperate refugees, we ate wild leaves and sucked water from the mud to survive. Afterward, we sold the few clothes we wore on our backs to local Nuer people in exchange for food in the areas where we spent the day. In July 10, 1987, we arrived in Ethiopia, half-starved and barely clothed with other orphans, many of whom became child soldiers. Soon we were taken by United Nations staff to Itang Refugee Camp which was the largest Refugee Camp in Ethiopia where most of the Sudanese refugees were at the time. Having crossed an international border, we were registered as refugees with the United Nations High Commissioner for Refugees in Ethiopia. The UN agencies appealed to the international community to help the Sudanese dying refugees and walking skeletons who had just arrived in the camp. We were housed in makeshift tents crowded by other refugees in Itang Refugee Camp. These tents became our home for the next five years, depending on food provided to us by the international community through the World Food Program of the United Nations (WFP).

My only memory of that refugee camp was that we found it to be a safe place where you could not hear the noise of weapons. There was neither electricity nor running water in the camp. We often walked twenty miles to fetch drinking and cooking water in the Gilo River. Before the war had displaced us from Southern Sudan, we were used to rearing herds of cattle and harvesting the crops that flourished every year in abundance. We didn't know anything like UN food aid or modern medicines. However, I learned about UN humanitarian aid when I reached Ethiopia where refugees heavily relied on foreign food aid and medicine which was never practiced in my homeland in Southern Sudan. In Itang Refugee Camp, food rations were distributed once every two weeks. Each refugee received four kilograms of maize or unmixed grain. We could eat only one meal a day or there would be nothing for the next day. Had it not been for the civil war, I would still be herding cattle or farming today in my rural community in Southern Sudan. There was limited freedom of movement of the refugees in the camp. Being a refugee limited your freedom of eating and freedom of higher education. In order to leave the camp and enter the neighbouring cities, the refugees had to get permission, and, therefore, the refugees were not allowed to work in the surrounding cities to earn money.

As for my education, I started school on the 15th of November, 1987 in Itang Refugee Camp in Ethiopia. The Refugee Schools in Ethiopia were taught in English. We began our lessons by writing letters and numbers with our fingers on the dirt floor. Our first chalkboards were actually made of cardboard and coal served as chalk. Finally, the United Nations High Commissioner for Refugees provided chalks and blackboards. I continued my studies in the Refugee Camp in Ethiopia until we were expelled by the new Ethiopian government in May 1991.

In 1990, I was employed with the World Food Programme as a pay list clerk in the refugee camp where I was paid not in currency but in biscuits and dinner invitations. My work was to call the names from the list for those refugees who would receive their food rations in the camp. It was a "work for food" program as the UN agencies used to call it in the Third World countries where refugees were working for food to keep them alive.

Chagai Chol Lual

Chapter 6

LEARNING TO COOK IN THE REFUGEE CAMP

As mentioned earlier, my mother taught me everything, including being equal to other people and caring for those who might need my help. But the one thing that my mother never taught me was cooking which was supposed to be the work of women or girls in our society. When we left our village we were assigned to Nyanber Monyluak Ayuel, as our guardian in order to take care of our needs in the absence of our mothers. She was a surrogate mother who was assigned by my half brother Dhieu Kiir Lual to take us under her wing. However, Nyanber Monyluak Ayuel, who had a constant, quick temper, was coming from Paweny clan from Dinka Padang community where their women were always barmy and more aggressive than a lioness. She was the estranged wife of my half brother Dhieu Kiir Lual who was in the war zone as SPLA commander at the time. Before our departure for Ethiopia, my half brother Dhieu Kiir Lual had firmly warned me against going to join the military services at the conscription Training Centre in Bilpam where many young boys of my age were being trained as child soldiers by the Sudan People Liberation Army (SPLA). Being an obedient child since day one, I decided to remain a civilian and study in school as requested by my half brother Dhieu Kiir Lual. This was in 1987 but in 1988, things changed automatically after the arrival of Mrs. Achol Thon Both. Madam Achol is the first wife of my half brother Dhieu Kiir Lual, who was the envy of the women among his eight wives. She messed up the situation within two weeks of her arrival from South Sudan. She informed Nyanber Monyluak Ayuel that the sons of Chol Lual Kiir and the son of Dol Kiir Lual would not help her in the future when they had finished their education because she said that these boys will only help their own families when they grow up. These words went to the ears of the distraught Nyanber Monyluak Ayuel without hesitation. The information she received from Achol Thon Both made her look and behave like a traditional magician woman I had seen previously. Shortly, she called a meeting to inform us that she was not going to cook for us as usual. She told us that she had been strongly advised by her co-wife Mrs. Achol Thon Both to not bother herself by cooking for us because she said that when we grew up we would just help our own mothers, not her. The disillusioned Nyanber Monyluak had regretted that she had wasted her valuable time by cooking for us while we were only going to help our own mothers when we grew up. (This short-tempered woman, however, was one of the first people I sent assistance to upon my arrival in Canada)

The news hit us like a brick but without a doubt I told my younger brother Dhot Chol Lual and my cousin Dhal Dol Kiir to take it easy and to leave this work to me as their guardian. I was the boy who took the burden of responsibility for my younger brother Dhot and my cousin Dhal on my shoulders. Nyanber was the first woman we had lived with and it took me a while to get used to cooking. Now we were parentless and became known to the world as one of the Lost Boys of Sudan. When Nyanber Monyluak Ayuel refused to cook for us, our hope was almost blown. But I felt that I had no choice but to learn to cook in order to avert the state of the starvation with these innocent children who were under my responsibility. The United Nations staff provided dishes and an iron pot for cooking.

I was completely inexperienced cook. I hated cooking because of sitting near an open smoky fire. In addition, before the war assaulted my culture, Dinka boys and men were not allowed to cook or appear anywhere near the kitchen where women were cooking. I was the first Dinka boy among the lost boys of Sudan to deal with this culture shock in the refugee camp in Ethiopia. One evening when it was my first time to cook, I thought I had prepared a special dinner of unmixed meal. But none of us could eat it. A dog came and I offered it to him. He inhaled it, then shook his head and walked away. It reminded me that the food was raw yet it did not bother me because cooking was primarily considered the work of women and girls, not for men or boys like me before the war disrupted our rich culture. In reality, I preferred herding cattle than cooking. The following evening, I attempted to cook another meal but when I took the cooking pot out of the fire, it appeared that the food was raw and tasteless, coupled with the fact that I had forgotten to add the salt!

TESTING THE BOILING WATER WITH MY HAND

I could boil water and once I tried to put the wheat flour into the water. It took me half an hour and I burned all the pot, let alone myself. I did not think how quickly I would be in charge of cooking, and I was the victim of my own negligence after I put my right hand into boiling water to see whether the water was boiling or not, but the already-boiled water severely burned my right hand. As I frantically withdrew my bare fingers, some of my burning skin remained on the pot and my hand began to bleed. I was in excruciating pain and the bleeding almost killed me. Later I traveled by foot to seek medical attention and I was diagnosed with severe burns. I still have the scar of this burn on my hand to this day. As a result of that burn, I missed two weeks of schooling, and I did not get good marks at the first term examination. I still remember the endeavour I made to catch up with the class after I had returned to school. Math and religion were the hardest subjects for me. In spite of these difficult times, I was proud and cheerful at the final examination where I passed grade three with good marks and high spirits.

Cooking continued to be a problem, but I learned how to cook through several attempts, though it was a slow process. As the cook, I had a great deal of responsibility with cooking, collecting fire wood for cooking and cleaning the dishes, as well as washing the clothes. I used to cook on an outdoors with a cooking pot. When my younger brother Dhot and my cousin Dhal came home for dinner, my plan of giving them food prior to cooking it was to walk off and wash the clothes. As a novice, I still had a lot to learn and this is where I realized the difference between cooking food and cooking soup. But I kept on cooking the food only without furthering this little knowledge to another level. In addition, I had no interest in learning how to cook soup. Finally, I attempted a simple, poorly cooked meal. The boys were very happy with me and praised me that I was a good cook. All we ate was unmixed meal and we drank the milk that the UN staff had given us.

I was tired all the time because I had no rest when I came from school. We were staying in our small tent where I would wash my dishes in my hands because there was neither a bathtub nor a kitchen in the camp. Cooking and washing dishes were so time consuming when I could have been using those hours to study or do home work. Instead it was cook or starves. I struggled like this until my dear mother Nyanbuny came from Sudan and caught up with me in 1991. That meant I had experience in cooking for three years.

I still recall the time when my food was burned into ashes. Sometimes I would rush my food out of the fire while it is still raw but we used to laugh over that mistake before we ate the food that was poorly cooked. We liked such food because it was either eats such raw food or face starvation. To fuel our anger, the estranged Nyanber Monyluak Ayuel with Achol Thon Both who had refused to cook for us earlier would laugh at us every night when we were eating our food and they used to tell their neighbours that those hungry boys are eating lightly-cooked food. The merciless women would sit wide-eyed, their faces wreathed in big smiles as we somehow managed to eat our food. I have no idea why these pitiless women were so adamant on upsetting our dinner just as we were beginning to eat. I often ignored their laughing because they could have helped us.

Meanwhile, my half brother Dhieu Kiir Lual who had inspired me to have an education, was in the war zone as commander in the Sudan People Liberation Movement/Army SPLM/A where he was fighting for the liberation of Southern Sudan against the ruthless Islamic regime in Khartoum who were mistreating the Southerners as if they were not Sudanese. My half brother Dhieu Kiir Lual was a strong believer in freedom and remained in peace with officers under his command. But he is also a proud and stubborn man who responds to affronts to his dignity with rage. When humiliated, he would lash out to his opponents with a strong tone like his late uncle Wuor Lual Kiir. My personal relationship with him was as close as twins. We understand each other without any doubt. He would often consult me about family matters. He had eight wives and scores of children, excluding the children of his countless concubines. Most of his wives were so jealous, as if they were born and raised in the Shilluk Kingdom where jealousy is believed to bring glorification in heaven. My half-brother Dhieu also enjoyed a good bottle of wine and the company of attractive women, just like some of his fellow comrades in the SPLM/A movement.

My half brother Dhieu Kiir Lual was in Abuong as overall commander of the SPLA forces in 1986 to 1988 before he had handed the overall leadership of Upper Nile zone to Dr. Lam Akol Ajakwin. After the handover, my half-brother remained as commander of Abushok Task Force. Some of those who had been among his most trusted officers from Ngok Lual Yak clan were the first enemies to betray him to the serial killer, the late Akim Aluong whom Dr. Lam Akol Ajawin used to kill the SPLA officers of Padang community. My half brother Dhieu Kiir Lual was falsely accused of corruption and misconduct by late Monylang Agok Monyjok. This accusation led to his imprisonment and ouster as commander of Abushok Task Force by Dr. Lam Akol Ajakwin. After this, he was jailed and endured pitiless circumstances in the prison under the atrocious rule of the late Akim Aluong with the support of the few conspirators of Ngok Lual Yak officers who aspire to take his position. The entire Ajuba community brought one hundred head of cattle as surety to Akim Aluong in order to release my half brother Dhieu Kiir Lual from jail. According to my half brother Dhieu Kiir Lual, he said that he was accused by certain officers in the SPLA movement of mismanagement in order to thwart his rising military clout. Had it not the involvement of Abushok task forces under the fierce resistance of now Police Brigadier Aluong Gach Awan and the late captain Nyok Ret Bayek, my half brother Dhieu Kiir Lual would have been killed by Akim Aluong just as Daniel Akol Chol, better known as Akol Ayen, who was killed for nameless reasons by Akim Aluong with the support of some traitors in exchange for promotion. The SPLA martial court later exonerated my half brother Dhieu Kiir Lual for lack of evidence. Afterward, he was released from detention after nearly nine months in the prison. His personal friendship with Mr. Aluong Gach Awan remained firm throughout this ordeal. Later, that allegation overshadowed his promotion during his ensuing military career in the SPLM/A movement until the signing of the Peace Agreement in Sudan. After the Comprehensive Peace Agreement, he was effectively appointed as Commissioner of Baliet County for two years and remained an active member of the SPLM party. Soon after his release, he came to Ethiopia to stay with us for one month before he was transferred to the front line in Southern Blue Nile with his forces. Upon his arrival in Itang, he delegated our guardianship to his fifth wife Alal Chol Nyang as our next surrogate mother instead of Nyanber Monyluak Ayuel.

We were relieved to have Alal Chol Nyang as our surrogate mother in an atmosphere where food was only the tool people were relying on. Madam Alal Chol Nyang took her new assignment with her whole heart for a few months before she was taught to hate us once again by the same merciless women who were surrounding her. The goals of these jealous women were to discourage us enough to drop out of school, but none of us had given up the hope of going to school.

At first Madam Alal Chol Nyang worked really hard to help us by cooking our food and washing our clothes. After approximately four months, she changed her mind and behaved like a drunken person as she used some rude remarks. This act made me feel hopeless toward the wives of my half brother Dhieu Kiir Lual who seemed to be practicing jealousy in vain. In spite of these circumstances, I was somehow able to graduate from elementary school with high marks.

Before my departure for Ethiopia, my brother half Dhieu Kiir Lual had instructed me to go to Ethiopia, and along with his wife as a guardian. Also, he sent along with us his body guards Mr. Bol Machol Jok and the late Captain Awan Yai Kac, who was our nephew, to stay with us in Itang Refugee Camp in Ethiopia.

These trustworthy men really supported us through many ways and I will never forget their support.

Bol Machol Jok is still appreciated by many people, including myself, for his passion and hospitality. His interest and persistent encouragement were necessary qualities for us during those early days in Ethiopia. He helped me enormously with his strong advice to get my education in Itang refugee camp. Mr Bol Machol Jok himself was the Chieftain of Adong section before he joined the Sudan People Liberation Army (SPLA) in 1984 to fight for the freedom of Southern Sudan. As such, his words were always full of legitimacy and that is why I still trust him to the present. Bol Machol Jok used to encourage us to read and write although he himself was illiterate. Currently, he is a captain in the Sudan People Liberation Army known as SPLA in Southern Sudan.

Since the beginning of the civil war in 1983, many young boys of my age, including the so-called Lost Boys of Sudan, had been volunteered to go to the front line as child soldiers. Two years later, I met Mr. Chigai Miyom Wuor in the refugee camp in Ethiopia after nearly seven years without seeing one another. Chigai Miyom Wuor is one of the men from home who were from Bango in Ajuba area where we all belonged. He was slightly older than me by age but not enough older to claim the special place of an elder of the community. In Dinka culture people sit according to age in the community. If there are others older than you, you still cannot have a place as an elder until there is room. The elders represent the younger men, and only the elders have a voice in community affairs.

As a man of justice and equality since childhood, Chigai Miyom Wuor had decided to join the SPLA movement in 1985 and volunteered to fight for the freedom of Southern Sudan in particular and Sudan in general for the sake of freedom in the whole country. He was badly wounded and lost his left arm in 1989 in Kurmuk in Southern Blue Nile where he was deployed as part of his military duty. I was shocked when I first saw him without one arm in Itang Refugee Camp in 1989. But being the fearless man he was, he reassured me to forget his missing arm, as I trembled with tears. My friend Chigai Miyom Wuor is a very truthful man, and I had grown close to him. I had built up ties of trust and friendship with him and his support was particularly significant to me. After all, he was the man whose views I respected. We could be separated for a month, but when we met again we would resume our conversation as if it had never stopped. He was not a talkative man though he carried inside him vast reserves of sympathy for his friends and families. A number of friends were there in the camp with us including Chol Lok Mabek, who used to entertain us with funny jokes in the camp. He spoke oral English very well, better than the school boys, even though he did not know how to write or read in English. Another friend, the late Ayiei Tuong Garang was a man of high morals, but his intention always was to go to the war zone as an SPLA soldier which he did in 1990 and was killed by the enemy around Juba. Mr. Gat Lok, as we used to call him, was an SPLA soldier but he went to the front line in 1990 to fight for the freedom of Southern Sudan. He is believed to be still alive and is a Captain in the SPLA force in Southern Sudan.

In the evening, we would share peacefully hearty jokes, as well as food, in the refugee camp where food was very rare. The conditions that we experienced during those years in the refugee camp in Ethiopia drew us ever closer together and we truly grew to treasure our friendships to the point where we trusted each other without reservation. Many of my childhood friends, including those who were with me in Itang Refugee Camp, have died in the civil war in Southern Sudan, or have been displaced and become refugees. The rest were involved in the long enduring struggle until the signing of the Comprehensive Peace Agreement in 2005 in Sudan between the Government of Sudan and the Sudan People Liberation Movement at this time.

EMOTIONAL REUNION WITH MY MOTHER

My mother received word in Sudan from friends that we were in a state of near starvation in an Ethiopian refugee camp.

The news made my mother lose a few pounds from her already skinny body because she was worrying about her orphans, as she used to call us. After a few weeks, my mother arrived in Ethiopia with my sister Nyanyiik Chol Lual. We were reunited with our mother Nyanbuny and our sister Nyanyiik in March 1991 at Itang Refugee Camp in Ethiopia after nearly five years of being separated. I first caught sight of my mother who seemed to be older than when I left her in Sudan in early 1987, but my youngest brother Dhot totally did not recognize my mother because he expected my mother would have looked the same as the time he left her in Southern Sudan. In reality our mother looked too old and too skinny for him to recognize her.

It was the first time we had seen our mother in five years and she raced to greet us by spitting on our foreheads as a sign of greeting and traditional blessing. In Dinka culture you can neither shake the hands of your mother nor look straight into her eyes like what we do here in Western countries. The Dinka elders are second to none, thus they are treated with dignity. My mother would have been in her early fifties now but she looked extremely older than that. When my younger brother Dhot recognized her he immediately ran and hugged her, choking back tears. She sprinkled water on our heads and shoulders in a tribal blessing. It was an emotional reunion with our mother. None of us knew that the other ones were alive.

Our joyful reunion was exciting and we had so much catching up to do. My mother told us many things about our families back home and also about the events that had taken place since our separation, including the death of our maternal grandmother Arop Monyjok Reth. When I heard the news about the death of my maternal grandmother who helped my mother to raise us, my heart felt like it would rip itself from my chest and fly to where she had been buried. In my grief I wondered and I wished that my maternal grandmother could live so that I could repay her for the efforts that she had made to help us. The death of my maternal grandmother hit me like a ton of bricks, but my mother comforted me by saying that her mother was an awesome woman and her spirit will be with us forever. She was a loving trustworthy and wonderful grandmother who was always willing to adjust to the varying circumstances we had faced together. I loved my late grandmother, Arop with all my heart. She was honest and thoughtfulness. Being her grandson was golden as the sunset and a privilege I will never forget. My mother and my sister were registered as refugees in order to be eligible for food ration distribution. We had an amazing time in the refugee camp in Ethiopia where the weather was so enjoyable. In the refugee camp, we ate cornmeal and beans once a day for nearly five years without any complaint.

Chapter 7

RETURNING TO THE WAR ZONE IN SOUTHERN SUDAN

After almost five peaceful years in the refugee camp in Ethiopia, the United Nations officials in the camp told us that we must flee because the camp was going to be attacked by Ethiopian rebels. The only choice for us was to escape back into Sudan and die in our own country instead of running to another country, like Kenya. Soon we were chased back across the crocodile-infested Gilo River on May 25, 1991 by rampaging Ethiopian rebel soldiers. The line-up went for days along the banks of the Gilo River, swollen by bitter rain and heavy mud. Many people tried swimming in the water, but some drowned because they did not know how to swim and others were eaten by the crocodiles. Yet Ethiopian rebels with automatic rifles were chasing us, firing at the SPLA soldiers and those they viewed as SPLA child soldiers among the desperate fleeing refugees. During the evacuation I was planning to go with Alal Chol Nyang, the wife of my brother Dhieu Kiir Lual to join a group of refugees to travel to where my mother and siblings were. On the evening before I was to leave, my mother turned up. I did not know where I would have ended up if I had gone with the other group. Some 300,000 of us were heading to Sudan and we all survived the air bombardment from the government of Sudan. We walked hundreds of miles to Southern Sudan with nothing but the clothes we wore on our backs. This was due to the departure of Ethiopian president Mengistu Haile Mariam on May 21, 1991 and the approach of rebel forces about to take over the country, forces that were hostile to the Sudanese refugees in Ethiopia. The Sudanese refugees were evacuated from Ethiopia on May 25, 1991 and suffered starvation and ambushes on their way to Nasir town in Southern Sudan. Upon learning of our return, the Sudanese government ordered twice-a-day bombing raids on us on our way back to Sudan. The first groups of the Sudanese refugees who were streaming into Sudan soil were bombed by the Sudanese air force on their way before the United Nations warned the government of Sudan against their air bombardment on the Southern Sudanese refugees. The Red Cross workers provided transportation assistance for some of the sick, elderly and the disabled, though Gajak Nuer bandits shot and killed several refugees along the way and looted their possessions. Our group was guarded by the spear master and fortune-teller Mr. Duot Ahecmach, who would predict the situation to see whether or not we would meet any Nuer bandits on our way. Under his prophecy, we went peacefully through the Nuer villages without any confrontations with robbers on our way. It was awesome that the magician was helpful in this time of great need to offer the service of conjecture. I think that most of us in the group were Christians, except for my mother and other elders who were animists, but since it was something related to our safety, there was nothing wrong to gripe about his action. We were really grateful to Mr. Duot Ahecmach for his soothsaying throughout our journey, but we were still looking for another conjurer who could have foreseen the problem of food to deal with our hunger issue, but that conjurer did not show up. We arrived in Nasir town and just spent two days before we proceeded on our journey home to Ajuba area in Baliet County in the Upper Nile region.

COMING HOME AFTER FIVE YEARS IN EXILE

We trekked through dense forests and swamps to return home after five years in exile. The journey home took us two months of walking on a bumpy road to get to the remote village of Ajuba because of the bitter rains and heavy mud in the roads. We survived this journey by eating the fruits and wild leaves of the trees that we found in the forest, and we drank water from the holes in the ground. After many days on the way, we arrived in Dhiak area where we were graciously hosted for two days in the house of the late Chol Nyang, father in-law of my half brother Dhieu Kiir Lual, before we proceeded to Ayok village in

Ajuba area where our relatives were putting us up. The people of Dhiak section are very hospitable toward their guests. With modest provisions for themselves, they welcomed us with everything they had. As special guests of Chol Nyang and his family, we were welcomed with traditional honours. Each morning and night we were fed with a food mixed with cow butter and a plate full of meats, which included me eating a cock typically set aside for honoured traditional magicians, but none of the magicians could stomach the thought. In addition, I was overwhelmed by their hospitality and their generosity because they provided us lodging in their home for our entire two days stay.

After two days in Dhiak area, we proceeded with high spirits to Awier area to see my maternal aunt Akon Ayuel Koryom whom I thought was still alive. But to my grief, she was not. After our arrival in Awier area, Wal Chol Riak was so embarrassed that he did not know how to inform my mother about her sister. He had the look of a man besieged. I might have guessed that he did not even know we were coming. After a few minutes of silence, Wal Chol Riak took my mother aside and told her that her sister Akon Ayuel Koryom had passed away. My mother fell to the ground and began screaming. It was the news she had prepare herself to hear for years and she cried for a long while.

My reaction was to breathe deeply and wait before I could see where my maternal aunt was buried. After the death of my grandmother Arop Monyjok Reth it was the hardest news I had heard and I was really not prepared for it. The tears fell quickly from my eyes, as well as the rest of my siblings. My late maternal aunt Akon Ayuel Koryom was a few years younger than my mother and was too young to die. Though we had not seen each other for five years, she had been a big part of my life when I was a child. She was always amusing to be around and told me many traditional stories about our rich culture. In addition, she was the only maternal aunt I had in the world. Now I have no aunt or grandmother to whom I can go on this earth. After we had cried for a long time with our mother, we went to stand next to the grave of my late aunt to pay our respects. The death of my maternal aunt Akon Ayuel Koryom was a big blow to me personally because I was very close to her and our relationship was as two peas in a peapod. The memories of my maternal grandmother Arop and my maternal aunt Akon still bring tears to my eyes. As I grieved for my maternal aunt Akon and I thought about her only surviving son, Angui Dau Chol, who is now struggling on his own in Sudan to complete his university education. I pledged to support him financially to complete university, and I will continue to support him on his road to self sufficiency because he is like my brother Dhot and because his mother had helped my mother to raise us. Besides the immediate family of my mother, she was the only one still alive.

After three days to grieve in Awier, we headed off and walked the entire route to Ajuba area with our planned one-week journey to Ajuba becoming increasingly longer as we sought to avoid areas littered with land mines, cut through forests and waded across swamps. We arrived in Ajuba area on a chilly sunny morning for the first time in five years. We were directed by someone to Ayok village where our relatives were residing. Shortly before our arrival in Ayok village, we met the late Nyangieth Kuol Minyang, known to my mother as daughter of Kuol Nyanuer Monyjok. Imagine the joy when our relatives saw us set our feet on the ancestral land for the first time in five years. When Nyangieth saw my mother who was in front of me, she threw up her arms high over her head and shouted in Dinka language: "Wacwac aci ben, wacwac acie ben" meaning "My maternal aunt has come, my maternal aunt has come." As she recognized me behind my mother, she sobbed for a while as she kept calling my name with a trembling voice. I assured my late cousin Nyangieth Kuol that I was happy to see her once again. Her mother Athieng Ajuong Awuc and others, who were around appeared also, too overcome with emotion to speak. They thought I was lost and all the relatives were not aware that they would see me physically after so many years in exile as one of the Lost Boys of Sudan. In my own case I thought I was a refugee boy who was absent from the area, but my relatives insisted on calling me their lost boy. After a grueling two- months journey I was glad to be reunited with my relatives after such a long while.

Ajuba is the area mostly known for the sorghum crops but it could also be known for encouraging ecumenical spirit among the churches and traditional beliefs surrounded by the animists. Our relatives were living in thatched grass huts in the village of Ayok, a small farming community that had neither electricity nor running water. It was one of the remote areas accessible only by foot as it was raining and we walked on foot through the rain and mud. Each foot was carrying what seemed like fifteen pounds of mud. When we arrived in Ayok village, we were welcomed with open arms by our relatives who were rejoicing that we had arrived safely. The entire village came out to greet us with big smiles and warm hugs, as if we were long lost brothers and sisters. Before we entered into the traditional grass huts, my aged step mother Nyannyok Deng Ayoi, better known as Man Chuang Awuoldit, who was in charge of our family spirits, led us to the location sacred to our departed relatives under the tree in Ayok village, because it was believed to be the burial place of my grandfather Lual Kiir Arieu. We went there to praise our family spirits for our safe arrival. She had brought a cock and killed it in a traditional fashion by beheading under the tree where we were standing. She simply blessed the cock with the tribal prayer and then slaughtered it. After traditional prayers, then she poured water from a gourd onto our feet to purify us and bind us again to our ancestral village. Afterward, she spat on our foreheads in blessing for those who had disappeared and come back. Our relatives were filled with joy. They hugged us tightly and held our hands. After one week, our relatives arranged for a party of traditional home-made wine to celebrate our homecoming.

As mentioned at the onset, I spent almost five years in the refugee camp in Ethiopia. But moving to Southern Sudan meant going back to rural conditions similar to those in which I had lived before fleeing from civil war. The rainy seasons were especially hard, and sometimes we had to wade through swamps that reached up to our hips. We lived in a small traditional hut which was far from comfortable. Life in rural and remote area in Southern Sudan was primitive. We cooked on firewood in an open fire and we walked ten kilometers each way to fetch drinking water in the stream or nearby Sobat River. My refugee experiences in Ethiopia made it much easier for me to cope with the living conditions in Ayok as well as in other places that followed. After almost two weeks of reunions, I felt exhausted beyond description as I prepared to resume my farming activities in my village in Southern Sudan. Soon after I arrived in Ayok, I started to cultivate my own field. Upon my arrival in the area, I had to register with the SPLA movement as a former student. The SPLA officer told me that I was not allowed to go to Malakal city and I accepted their conditions because I was just a civilian and could not challenge the SPLA forces that were in control of the area.

In fact, the existing civil war in Southern Sudan was getting even worse, pushing us from one makeshift camp to another. Living in a war zone meant facing countless abuses and tortures without complaint. The area was full of unruly soldiers from various armed groups from the Sudan government and its allied militias who were a constant challenge. In addition, the SPLA forces were not free from abusing the powerless civilians in their territory even though some of the SPLA leaders in the movement were claiming to be fighting to restore the democratic system and sovereignty in the whole country.

One day my younger brother Dhot Chol Lual quarreled over the fishing in the Sobat River with one of the Ajuba nephews named Kach, better known as Kac Nyanjai. Kac was older than my brother Dhot by age. However, he beat up my brother to the extent that my half brother Dol Kiir Lual was furious. I approached Kac and tried to blame him for his ruthless act of fighting with such a small boy. Before I even finished my words, Kac ran to his uncle, the late Monytong Deng Lueth, who was the SPLA officer. He misinformed his uncle Monytong that I had almost beaten him. Late Monytong Deng Lueth then ordered his body guards to arrest me, and I received one hundred lashes on my bare back with branches of trees and rope. When I begged that you can not treated me like a criminal, he became infuriated and called his body guards who hastily escorted me to the prison and started to beat me up without any compassion. Shortly afterward I was jailed by the SPLA soldiers who were ordered by Monytong Deng Lueth in 1992. I was beaten severely once more in the prison after I tried to talk.

In the war zone, we were taught not to question anyone in a position of authority in the SPLA movement. Later on, Kac was beaten badly by my cousin Kiir Dhieu Kiir, better known as Thiep kuluit, as part of the retribution. But Ajuba elders intervened and the matter was resolved in Ajuba community, because my cousins were mobilizing to take further revenge particularly, my two cousins Dhal Dol Kiir and Kiir Dhieu Kiir who were angry at Kac for his betrayal. But who could question the mistreatment that I have received under the hands of the late Monytong Deng who was very powerful in his capacity as SPLA officer. In addition, the Ajuba men in the SPLA uniforms that were around during my abuse were either enjoying my mistreatment or were afraid to resist my ill-treatment. Were my fearless half-brother, the late Tor Wuor Lual still around, he would not endure to watch my mistreatment like this. But he was not there and I was abused by these pitiless SPLA soldiers like an Arab man. It was tense but I had to become used to these nervous situation in the war zone. The Sudan Armed Forces, as well as militias and SPLA troops, were used to terrorizing the civilians in Southern Sudan. The frequent beatings and inhumane treatment which I suffered in Southern Sudan at the hands of the Sudan Armed Forces, as well as its SSIM militias and SPLA forces, made me felt hopeless about my own life. During those terrible times of abuses and tortures, I did not think that I had much opportunity of staying alive. In reality, I was about twenty four years old, but because of my experiences I was much older than those of my age. The frequent beatings and inhumane treatment, coupled with seeing the dead bodies of my close friends during the massacre year in 1992 made me become like an extremely old young man. I was quite a fat young man with a big belly and jowly face. But after I was savagely beaten by the SPLA soldiers, my big belly and jowly face disappeared quickly.

At this time there were the enforced enlistments undertaken by the SPLA. The SPLA forces used to conscript the civilians for military training in the area and then send them to the front line. The civilians were forced to become soldiers without choice. The SPLA forces used to tell the civilians that they had no choice. Whether they liked it or not they had to contribute like the others who were volunteering to fight against the Islamic regime in Khartoum without any compensation. Those who were able to escape enlistment in the SPLA military during the civil war were not claiming their safety or their freedom from further conscription either because they were still being used as porters by the SPLA forces to carry the wounded soldiers or the heavy boxes of ammunitions on their heads, just like war prisoners. But being a porter was harder than being recruited to fight because you were vigorously required to carry the ammunition box heavier than one sack of sorghum. Moreover, the civilians were used as vehicles to carry the wounded SPLA soldiers, including the big- bellied ones, on their heads. I credited God for my survival in the war zone where many civilians were dodging the draft for the Arab war.

WAR WITHIN THE ENDURING CIVIL WAR

After we arrived in Sudan, we saw the devastation all around. The heartfelt traditional prayers I had heard from my relatives were deeply engraved on my mind even though I was never sure where I would end up. Despite the misery, we had hoped that the war would soon be over.

On August 27, 1991, three months after our arrival in Ayok village from Ethiopia refugee camp, a major split within the Sudan People Liberation Movement and Sudan People Liberation Army occurred over the leadership and direction of the movement in Upper Nile State, resulting in years of violence and bloodshed. The splinter groups were accusing the SPLM/A leader, the late Dr. John Garang Mabior of having a dictatorial fashion and broke away to form their own South Sudan

Independence Movement (SSIM) that took up arms against the SPLM/A movement in 1991. The breakaway factions were led by Dr. Riek Michar Teny, now Vice President of the Government of Southern Sudan and deputized by Dr. Lam Akol Ajakwin. Dr. Riek Machar Teny was trying to overthrow the SPLM/A leader, the late Dr. John Garang Mabior, in the name of reforming the movement to have democratic institutions and to improve its human rights records, but the self-declared reformer turned out to be the worst perpetrator of human rights abuse. As a result, Dr. Riek Machar Teny was trying to unseat the SPLM/A leader late Dr. John Garang Mabior, saying he was in a position to engineer enough defections from the movement to achieve his goal. Shortly after the split, the breakaway forces under Dr. Riek Machar Teny, managed to recruit the Nuer rowdy youth militants in different Nuer places and massacred thousands of innocent Dinka civilians in their villages. Dr. Riek Michar Teny encouraged the Nuer militants to sustain the uprising. After that he used his Nuer tribal militias to wage the war against the SPLM/A. In addition, he ordered the Nuer militants to chase and force the removal of one million Dinka people from their traditional land in Upper Nile State. As a result, the Nuer militants looted countless cattle from Dinka tribe and burned entire villages to the ground in Dinka land. This was the start of the worst period ever in the life of the Dinka Ngok Lual Yak people who were always caught in the crossfire between the Nuer militants and the SPLA forces.

On the other hand, the breakaway forces, mainly from the Shilluk tribe under the authority of Dr. Lam Akol Ajakwin, were terrorizing the Dinka Ngok villagers and pillaging their cattle. This split in the SPLM/A led to so much chaos and heavy fighting among Southerners in Southern Sudan resulting in the loss of countless lives from Nuer and Dinka tribes. Most of those who formed the South Sudan Independence Movement were of the belief that the SPLM/A was marginalizing them. After several months of fighting between the SPLA and the breakaway SPLA factions, mostly Nuer and Shilluk tribes, the breakaway factions turned to the Khartoum government for help.

The Islamic regime in Khartoum saw this as a way of diminishing the South Sudanese cause and jumped at the idea of partnering with the SSIM factions. The regime in Khartoum welcomed these factions with open arms and acknowledged them as the legitimate movement fighting for the aspirations of the South Sudanese people. Thus, in 1997 they signed the Khartoum Peace Agreement with the SSIM factions who then became elements of the Khartoum regime for a while. The Khartoum regime armed the Nuer militants to massacre the Dinka people, especially in Bor, in November 1991 where many Dinka people were killed. In reality, Dr. Riek Machar and Dr. Lam Akol Ajakwin were the most educated individuals in Southern Sudan; they were viewed by southerners as their future leaders due to their high level of education and leadership. But their failure to maintain order after their breakaway from the SPLM/A movement which resulted in tribal conflict in Southern Sudan reduced the people's trust in their ability to lead the nation thus it has put their future leadership into question. Later Dr. Riek Machar Teny was upset by the regime in Khartoum after the violation of their agreement and rejoined forces with SPLM/A, led by late Dr. John Garang Mabior, parting from Dr. Lem Akol Ajawin in the regime in Khartoum. Of course, this trick by the Khartoum regime did not result in a decline in the SPLA movement which was in control of the most towns in Southern Sudan and other marginalized areas, including the Nuba Mountains and Southern Blue Nile. After the Khartoum Peace Agreement, the Khartoum regime stepped up its support of the breakaway factions of the SPLA in an effort to divide further the Southern Sudanese people on tribal grounds and turn themselves against each other to achieve its political goals. The regime in Khartoum provided arms and ammunition to the Nuer militias to commit atrocities, including murder and arson in the Dinka villages in Southern Sudan. As a result of this split, the intertribal fighting between the Nuer and the Dinka tribes ensued, leading to the death of countless innocent citizens from these tribes in Upper Nile Region. Furthermore, the Nuer who formed the central part of the SSIM were butchering Dinka officers and soldiers who were deployed by the SPLM/A movement in the Nuer areas before the split. After the split, the Nuer militants were acting like wild cats because they were treating the Dinka as their first enemy rather than the Arabs of Northern Sudan who were the real enemies of the South. In response, the Dinka cornered the Nuer as a revenge for the killings of its people. This split led to tribal conflicts in which Nuer and Dinka shot, stabbed and burned each other alive. At this time Upper Nile State came under the iron grip of the South Sudan Independence Movement (SSIM). The SSIM forces quickly occupied the entire area in Baliet County, as well as my village of Ayok, to instigate attacks on SPLA forces. Ayok was in the iron grip of the Nuer insurgents and became the headquarters of Captain Jacob Gatwech Chol, better known as Gatwech Nyaguor.

Chagai Chol Lual

Chapter 8

SPLA ARMED FORCES ATTACK ON AYOK

After the split, the Nuer insurgents quickly occupied the entire area of Baliet County, including my village of Ayok, to launch attack on SPLA forces and take control of the SPLA-controlled areas. This was an attempt to drive out the SPLA freedom fighters from their bases. In October 1991, the SPLA armed forces, under the cover of darkness, with rocket-propelled grenades and assault rifles under the overall command of Cdr. George Athor Deng attacked the Ayok insurgency base in some of the heaviest forest fighting that the area has ever seen. The campaign to rid the Ajuba area of lawaless Nuer militias was ordered by Cdr. George Athor Deng to take place as scheduled. Cdr. George Athor Deng, whom the Nuer tribe feared most, was the SPLA zonal commander of the Upper Nile military command at the time. Cdr. George Athor was considered by many Nuer citizens to be the most powerful and feared figure in the Upper Nile region. Ayok was a village firmly in the hands of the Nuer militants, led by Captain Jacob Gatwech Chol, better known as Gatwech Nyaguor. Several explosions shook Ayok village in the attack that aimed to sweep away the insurgents in the area. During the attack, I was sleeping in my small hut while my mother and siblings were sleeping in the family hut. They fled separately in a crowd, terrified by the gunshots, but I ran away with the civilian population to the bush alone in a different direction. I finally met my mother and siblings after one day. All the families of Kiir Arieu were in the area that was attacked by the SPLA forces. Thankfully, none of them were killed, but several neighbours were badly injured. The SPLA forces were hunting for the insurgents who were camping in Ayok after the split within the SPLM/A. The Nuer militants were in control of Ayok and were mistreating the civilians in this area. The SPLA forces, under the overall command of Cdr. George Athor Deng, were opposing this and were trying to sweep out the Nuer militants in the whole area which they were occupying. We knew it was the SPLA because after they had captured the entire area they started shouting SPLA Oyee, SPLA Oyee. We heard the bullets fired by the SPLA, followed by the sound of the bombs thrown by the Nuer militants. Soon we had to flee into the forest and we survived only by walking into the wilderness. While hundreds of thousands were screaming and sobbing, however, civilians spilled out onto the forest in the shadow of the fabled Ngok land. The SPLA soldiers took cover behind a row of trees and exchanged gunfire with the Nuer insurgents, while petrified civilians dropped to the forest floor in an effort to elude the barrage of bullets undertaken by both the SPLA forces and the insurgents who callously asked to be called the white army. One SPLA soldier was killed by the Nuer insurgents in that attack and four Nuer insurgents were badly wounded, including the Nuer insurgency commander and his deputy, in the attack aimed to wipe away the Nuer insurgents in Ayok area. During this attack, six civilians were badly injured in the fighting. It was raining bullets as some people were sent to evacuate those wounded under attack, but failed against the onslaught of gunfire.

I went in one direction that day and my mother with my siblings went another way. It took me almost six hours before I learned whether any of them were alive. The exchange of the gunfire lasted from 4 am to 12pm. After the faltering effort to drive Nuer militias from Ayok, the SPLA forces withdrew from the area. When the sound of gunfire ended, we returned to our houses expecting the worst.

The body of a dead SPLA soldier was displayed in the centre of Ayok. The Nuer militants were controlling the area and they would not let the civilians bury the dead body and put it to rest. The Nuer militants put a letter on the dead body that said if anybody tried to bury the body then the militants would kill them too. The letter also stated that the militants would behead and display any Dinka civilian who tried to assist the SPLA forces.

After this attack, terrible times followed as civilians were killed and plundered on a daily basis. Most of our livestock were taken by force by the Nuer insurgents. After the SPLA had with-drawn, the Nuer militiamen came to our houses and told us not to work in our fields for five days. During these five days the government-sponsored Nuer insurgents called a meeting of all the chiefs and village elders. I went to this meeting with my chief to interpret for my chief from simple broken Arabic language into Dinka dialect. In the meeting they particularly warned us, the citizens of Ayok village. They said that they had told us the last time that if anything happened we would be held respon-sible. Now something had happened and they were going to take action. After this we went home and waited until the Nuer insurgents allowed us to return to farm in our fields. After ten days we were allowed back to work. The Nuer militiamen started arresting the people whom they suspected as SPLA supporters, because the Nuer and Dinka have been rivals for months after the split in the SPLM/A. The Nuer insurgents accused the Ngok Dinka of siding with the SPLA movement. The unruly Nuer mil-itants severely beat the Ajuba Chieftain who had refused to con-tribute girls to the insurgency commanders as their wives. This was brought to the awareness of Cdr. Chuang Michar Ajak, but all he did was to forgive the militants and continue with them as he found them helpful. This might have been the motive for the community protest in Ngok Lual Yak community who felt that Cdr. Chuang Michar Ajak was not doing enough to contest traitors in the Ngok Land. Local traitors did much chaos to their own people as they allied with the Nuer militants to arrest those whose daughters and nieces were married to the SPLA officers in the Ajuba area. My half brother Dol Kiir Lual was accused of being an SPLA collaborator by one of the well-known slanderers in the Ajuba area in hopes of his gaining the chieftainship that could be assigned to him by the radical Nuer insurgency com-mander in the area if he betrayed one of the citizens of Ajuba. He accused my brother Dol Kiir Lual of being an SPLA collabo-rator because some of the SPLA officers had family connections with our relatives, including the now SPLA Major Thon Tuong Akong who was the husband of my niece Apiny Wieu Miyom, and the SPLA captain, the late Nyok Ret Bayek, who was from

Banygo group where we were belonged. These accusations led
to many arrests but no charges of my half brother Dol Kiir Lual
and our relatives at that time. Since I was a young student coming from Ethiopia with some skills in English, I was ordered by
the militia to be their secretary in order to write letters that they
would send to their wives and girl friends in various Nuer rural
areas, because most of the Nuer militants were illiterate. Being
a secretary to these illiterate militants rescued me and my relatives from further arrest, although it was a challenging job because it dealt with the Nuer language and I did not know the
Nuer language properly, and the Nuer militants did not know
how to read or write. Even though we were not happy with the
militants, we had to give them food and cows, as well as homes
and girls. The civilians had no right to reject the needs of the
armed militants who would otherwise kill them like dogs.

In November 1991, the movement of Ngok Lual Yak citizens was restricted by Nuer militants, because many militants
became suspicious of us and even accused us of spying for the
SPLA. All these allegations were shown to be false but the Nuer
insurgents still suspected us of siding with the SPLA forces
who used to come and attack their bases frequently. At first we
thought that Cdr. Chuang Michar Ajak could work toward the
security of the whole population in Baliet County, but before
long he started running off. Cdr. Chuang Michar was more interested in traditional dances than in managing the affairs of
entire communities. Though he was a good speaker himself, he
was not serious enough about tackling the security facing the
entire Dinka Ngok Lual Yak community in the area. As a result the area was constantly full of traitors who were looking
for leadership to grab. There was also enormous hesitancy over
many issues that faced the communities. One example was the
arrest of some civilians in Ajuba area who were betrayed to the
Nuer militants by someone whose name was acknowledged by
the people of Ajuba. The Ajuba community elders sent the del-
egations to Cdr. Chuang Michar to persuade him to take action
against this individual, but he refused to do anything because it
seemed that he thought that some of the conspirators among the

community in Ajuba greater area would be useful cronies to him in his future struggle against some of the SPLA members in the Ajuba area who were accused of sustaining the SPLA movement rather than his breakaway factions. Our situation was difficult because the Nuer miltants were mistreating us and our leader, the late Cdr. Chuang Michar Ajak was not serious about the safety of his people.

THE SPLIT LEFT THE SECTARIAN HOSTILITY

The split within the SPLA/M contributed gravely to fuelling the sectarian violence between the two communities of Ngok Lual Yak and Dongjol clans who were fighting each other for political reasons. The SPLA forces and breakaway factions of both sides were on standby to deploy as feuds between the two clans of Ngok Lual Yak and Dongjol threatened to erupt into sectarian violence which occurred later. As a result of this atrocious split, the SPLA veteran, the late Nyok Ret Bayek, was killed in broad daylight in Wuol village in 1993 by merciless Dongjol militants. This split within the SPLM/A created the situation in which Dongjol people would kill Ngok Lual Yak people without mercy. In retaliation the Ngok Lual Yak people would kill the people of Dongjol without any forgiveness, resulting in the loss of many innocent lives from both sides.

Before the split, the two clans of Ngok Lual Yak and Dongjol in the Baliet County were living together peacefully as in the days before the war when there had been no clan conflict. In addition, the members of Padang community everywhere in Southern Sudan were also killing each others as a result of the split within the SPLM/A. Sectional fighting among the members of Ngok Lual Yak clan in the SPLM/A uniform were increasing as they had been already split up into two factions of their individual choice and then turned on each other. The breakaway factions were led by the late Cdr. Chuang Michar Ajak who was in favour of the so-called South Sudan Independence Movement (SSIM) which he supported until his death in Khartoum in

2002.

Meanwhile the forces loyal to the SPLA movement were led by Cdr. Makuac Akol Ayiei with the support of the entire community of Ngok Lual Yak clan. (Brigadier General Makuac Akol Ayiei is currently the Director of the Prisons Guard in Western Equatoria State in Southern Sudan.) However, Cdr. Makuac Akol Ayiei was backed by the SPLA forces under the overall command of Cdr. George Athor Deng (now a major General). Cdr. George Athor Deng was the man whom the Nuer people feared the most and was the strongest SPLA commander in the Upper Nile zone along with his forces, despite the presence of the insurgents in the entire area of the Upper Nile. He was widely spoken of in the army as a man with a promising future. He had a reputation as a courageous battlefield commander. His courage enabled him to earn a decoration for bravery in combat from the SPLA movement. The once-peaceful Baliet County became one of the most dangerous and volatile counties in the Upper Nile state with the SPLA forces and breakaway forces that were fighting against each other.

FIGHTING THE NUER MILITANTS IN AJUBA

On the 10th of April, 1992, a week before the Nuer militants attack on Ngok citizens was scheduled, the SPLA forces under the overall command of Cdr. George Athor Deng attacked the insurgent bases and shot the factional Nuer militants en masse for the second time in Bil Akong and Wune Ding areas in Ajuba area, sparking a four-day battle between SPLA forces and Nuer insurgents. We awoke to find the entire village of Bil Akong surrounded by the SPLA soldiers in uniform. They were looking for Nuer militants in the area whom they started to shoot one by one. This attack had somewhat traumatized us. The fighting between the SPLA forces and Nuer militias in Bil Akong village quickly spread, engulfing Wune Ding and other insurgent bases throughout Baliet County. I woke up to great turmoil and ran to the yard. Terrified residents were caught in the crossfire and they were running from it like bees from a burning hive. After the SPLA fighters took over several villages in Baliet County, there were cruel retributions and the mass murders that took place during that day are still etched in my mind. We crawled out with the ring of flying bullets overhead. After several hours of artillery and gunfire, the SPLA had control of the area of Bil Akong and the entire Dinka Ngok land. The SPLA forces instructed area residents to remain in their homes and said that they did not intend to harm any civilians. Later, we were told by the SPLA soldiers that the Nuer militants were planning to attack and kill the Dinka Ngok Lual Yak citizens in the middle of April 1992. Happily, they did not succeed in their plans. The SPLA briefly overran several areas in Baliet County for one month, but then fell back as they ran out of ammunition.

Bil Akong village was and is still a holy hotspot for all Ajuba people since they would gather in Bil Akong village to give thank to Akong spirits for giving them everything, including grain and health. Ajuba women used these words when things got out of hand: "Akong ting thon guote biong" in Dinka dialect which means "Woman who is powerful in spirit." Since then, the Nuer insurgent forces, with the help of the Sudan Armed forces stepped up a new attack that aimed to sweep out both the SPLA forces and the Dinka Padang in Baliet and Korfulus Counties, because the Nuer insurgents accused two clans of the Dinka tribe, namely the Ngok Lual Yak and Luac Akok Wieu, of siding with the SPLA movement. The fighting between the SPLA and the SSIM militants went on for one month before the withdrawal of the SPLA forces. The Nuer militants were strongly supported by the regime in Khartoum in an attempt to foil the SPLA movement which the Islamic ruling regime in Khartoum had condemned as an infidel movement. This response from both the Sudan Armed Force and its allies forced the SPLA to withdraw its forces in the Baliet area. Without their protection we moved to the bush and slept in dense forest to avoid militant attacks. Water became rare because it was the dry season. Most animals were gone except for lions, hyenas and vultures that always hovered above the sky, waiting. If you sat under the tree to rest, the vultures thought that you were dead and they would come down and sit close by because they were used to finding corpses in the grasses and under the trees.

Chapter 9

THE SPLA SOLIDIER ORIGINATES A STAMPEDE

There were many attacks against people who were pre-sumed to have water and food in the dry forest. One of the SPLA soldiers created a stampede by firing many bullets in the air in the forest while he knew exactly that the civilians were around in the bush, fearing for their lives from the Nuer militants. Shortly after the shots, people ran into different directions in the for-est thinking that the Nuer militants had attacked them. I was amongst these desperate civilians and I was almost separated from my mother and siblings during this stampede, but I was able to reunite with them and other relatives within a matter of twenty minutes, although the water we had saved was stolen by this pitiless soldier. After the stampede, he spotted our water in the gourds and he stole them. We survived by drinking our own urine for the next four days. For the first time I saw people dy-ing of thirst while others were dying of hunger. After these days, many people were screaming and dying of thirst in the forests.

My half brother Dol Kiir Lual, who loved his own life more than that of his own children, was the first person to flee the scene by himself to Anakdiar where he reported to our rela-tives there that we might have been killed by Nuer militants. The reaction of my relatives was about to cause a split within the great families of Lual Kiir Arieu. My half brother Monytong Wuor Lual said that if Chagai was alive and the rest of the rela-tives were killed then it would be okay. My dear half brother Monytong was just caring for my own life rather than that of the whole family of twenty persons who accompanied me. My late half brother Tor Wuor Lual reacted in anger by nearly attack-ing his brother Monytong Wuor Lual for his comment, claiming that the spirits of all our family members were the same and that one person among the relatives should not be mourned above the rest of the same family members. My half brother late Kon Mamor Lual ,who was a prominent figure in the government of Upper Nile state, was heading to Anakdiar from Malakal to provide food aid to those who had arrived in Anakdiar with nothing. My late half brother Kon Mamor Lual almost fainted and had to be escorted sobbing to the guest house in Anakdiar after he had learned from my half brother Dol Kiir Lual that I might have been killed by Nuer militia along with a number of relatives. My late half brother Chuang Ayom Lual who was in Anakdiar Displaced Camp was in shock with terrible headaches as a result of the news of my presumed death with the rest of the relatives. The entire relatives were worrying about our fate and it distressed them greatly.

WAGING WAR AGAINST THE DINKA

After the withdrawal of the SPLA, the rival Nuer militia, the Southern Sudan Independence Movement (SSIM) led by Commander Dr. Riek Machar Teny, attacked the entire area in Baliet County, shooting randomly in the villages and kept chasing the Dinka civilians like deer chased by dogs. The Arabs were not only killing people with guns but also were actively mobilizing people to kill each other. The regime in Khartoum was encouraging Nuer militias to mobilize the masses to kill the Dinka people. The Sudan Armed Forces and its militias would force people to give up their own thoughts and beliefs, making them die like dogs without dignity. They would use both guns and sticks to kill the people in Southern Sudan because they said that the frightening deaths would encourage the Arabs and Nuer followers to continue their practice of killings. Therefore, the vengeful Nuer militants used this method to kill the Dinka people. The Nuer and Dinka rivalry had escalated from tribal animosity to a government counter-insurgency strategy whereby the Nuer become the government proxies against the Dinka whom they perceived to be the backbone of the SPLM/A. We fled to the forest where we were scavenging for food and water in the forest, almost starving. We were like deer trying to flee the lions.

The White Army, the militia commanded by radical Nuer prophet Wud Nyang Gatkek, was involved in the clashes that lasted for about four hours before dawn. Wud Nyang Gatkek declared himself Prophet of the Nuer tribe in Southern Sudan soon after the split within the SPLM/SPLA in 1992. The Nuer prophet had been recruiting and training young men in groups known as the White Army to wage war against the Dinka. These groups were armed and taught by their prophet that the Dinka were their enemies. These rogue Nuer militants were supported by the Khartoum regime to shoot the Dinka civilians in their villages like animals. Many civilians were captured and killed in that attack while some people were dying of thirst and starvation. I saw many dead people for the second time in my life. Some wild animals, such as foxes and cats, became good eaters of the flesh, let alone the vultures who were celebrating while people were mourning. The Nuer militants were chasing us with loud voices shouting: "Catch, catch the Dinka peoples and kill them without mercy because our borders with the Dinka people have no forgiveness to declare."

THE FORCEFUL INVASION OF DINKA NGOK LAND

After the Nuer militias had taken control of the Ngok areas they gave up chasing us. At this time, the militants were on the land of my ancestors and invited their Nuer fellow citizens in Nuerlands to come over and occupy the Ngokland which the Nuer had yearned to seize, claiming that the land of Dinka Ngok had been blessed by God with enough food for everyone. The regime in Khartoum supported the militants' move and urged their friendly forces, as they called them, to step up attacks across Ngokland, including the use of shelling bombs. The so-called Naath civilians and their cold-hearted killers fully invaded our land and joyfully ate all kinds of the crops, including the millet and maize that the Dinka Ngok citizens had stored in their countless barns. To make matters worse, the self-declared Nuer prophet, Wud Nyang Gatkek, claimed that he was God and that he possessed power by God to make the Dinka people fly out of their native soil like birds. As a result, the self-described prophet formed the White Army forces of mostly youths and cattle rustlers from the whole clan of Nuer tribe. He then called for the mass killing of the Dinka tribe by all means. People heard his words as of the only God. He recruited and mobilized his native Nuer followers and deployed them in Ngok land in order to kill the Dinka people. The self-declared Nuer Prophet instructed his followers to concentrate their attack on the Dinka rather than other tribes in Southern Sudan. The majority of Nuer citizens were still drunk on the lies of their prophet Wud Nyang Gatkek, who had been telling them that anyone killed after this holy war against the Dinka, would have a great chance to go to heaven and later rise up in their byres like Jesus Christ. Wud Nyang was treated as the only true prophet by the Nuer tribe. The Nuer men obeyed him without hesitation while the Nuer women fell into his arms to glorify him as an angel. None of his promises materialized nor did any one get killed during this tribal conflict rise again from the death. The self-declared prophet Wud Nyang falsely presented himself as an angel and had been lying for six years before his beheading in February 2006 by his former Nuer followers in Yuai along with many others. It seemed clear that it was the White Army and other lawless Nuer groups mainly from Lou Nuer who killed Prophet Wud Nyang Gatkek because they believed him to be a traitor for joining the SPLA movement. The Nuer borrowed the word from Arabs in Khartoum who used to say that when you killed a Dinka man or woman then you had a great chance to go to heaven without delay.

I escaped with my family and relatives to the bush where we wandered from place to place looking for help, surviving by hiding in the forest. The government-sponsored militias descended on various Dinka Ngok areas one night and started setting huts on fire. Terrified elderly and sick people who were unable to run were burned alive in their huts. Others died as they struggled to break out of their huts and free themselves from the fire. Many people who were hiding in the dry forest withered from hunger and thirst there while others were devoured by lions or killed by militants. The conflicts amounted to ethnic cleansing and citizen eviction. For several hours explosions rained shells and debris over a radius of three kilometers, causing panic in the area. The sound of the gunfire fueled fear and throngs of terrified, stricken people poured into the bush, not knowing where they were heading. In the evening darkness, hundreds of people, including many hysterical children, ran into the crocodile-infested Sobat River. As a result, many people were eaten by the crocodiles. Some people drowned because they did not know how to swim while the children were snatched by the rushing water. Those who fled to the waterless forests faced the lack of water and food. I was among the groups that were in the dried up forests. One cup of water would be shared by several people because if you drank it all, then some people were going to die. However, after days without water, we drank our own urine in order to sustain our lives. If we had not drunk our own urine, then we would have died like the rest of our friends.

Chagai Chol Lual

Chapter 10

DISPLACED WITHIN MY OWN COUNTRY

After hiding in the impenetrable forests for three weeks, we then fled to the neighbouring Shilluk Kingdom where we took up residence in Anakdiar Displaced Camp. Our groups arrived in the middle of the night when it was completely dark. Despite the darkness, the SPLA officers who escorted the civilians ordered our group to cross a river by boat. We could see neither the river nor the boat. Still, we groped around until we stumbled upon a boat and although scared, we managed to make our way across the river. Once on the other shore, we headed for a star light that was visible over the nearby village of Anakdiar where we found a few trees. This was to be our new home for the next five months. It was a sprawling camp with a population of about five hundred thousand people, mostly Dinka Ngok and Luac communities who were displaced from their homeland by militants in Baliet and Korfulus Counties. When we arrived in Anakdiar, we were put in one place by the local city officials where we had to be registered as Internally Displaced Persons. Internally Displaced Persons are fundamentally refugees but inside their own country. The only difference between Internally Displaced Persons and refugees are that the refugees have crossed an international border and have met the criteria for support from the United Nations and other international support organizations. Many people from Ngok Lual Yak and Luac communities were arriving in Anakdiar on a daily basis and the regional officials in Malakal, including my late half brother Kon Mamor Lual, were trying to help us in Internally Displaced Camp by providing lentils. We had almost nothing to eat, just a small amount of lentils that the regional government provided but there were no shelters. We cooked in the open with metal pots over smoky fires but we did not have enough food or firewood. It was the hottest month of May and the place was like a hell. The ground burned our feet as we ran from tree to tree for shade during the day.

I could not believe that I would be a refugee in my own land, but it happened to me. The UN agencies did not arrive until several weeks later. After three weeks, the World Food Program brought us individual ration packs but after that they brought us food which we divided up between ourselves. There was not much food but there was enough to keep us alive. We were put in a place called Ruot wat by the local Municipality to stay away from the residents. It was a wide, open sprawling wasteland where tens of thousands of human beings slept in the open, lying down on a dirty rough floor with almost no material possessions except for the soiled clothes they wore on their backs. Many people were living in the open; a few people had trees, while others found refuge in hastily constructed huts made of grass to cover their heads. I was able to build our grass hut with the help of my mother after nearly three weeks without a roof over our heads. Our hut was very small but we just needed a roof overhead, a safe place for displaced persons to lay their heads. It was a wide open field but our living in the camp was like living in an open prison because we were not free to leave the camp. When we asked to leave we were told by the municipal officials that we were not allowed to visit Malakal or go anywhere in case we took cholera with us to the city. As mentioned earlier, the World Food Program provided us with food and set up a clinic for patients, but the water was foul and sanitation was non-existent. Apart from these meager activities, the people in the displaced camp were living off monthly food rations given by the World Food Program. It was difficult with one meal a day or sometimes every other day. Internally Displaced People were entirely dependent on the goodwill of the international community to address their needs. I thought that I would never become a refugee in my own state like Upper Nile but it turned out that I was about to starve in a displaced camp in my own country.

HORRIBLE LIFE IN ANAKDIAR INTERNALLY DISPLACED CAMP

In April 1992, more than five hundred thousand displaced people crossed into neighboring Shulluk Kingdom and settled in near the town of Anakdiar. There were dead bodies floating in the water below and feces were everywhere. The outside air reeked of urine and feces. Inevitably conditions in the hastily set-up camps were appalling. Two weeks later, cholera hit the camp and ran rampant throughout the community. In the second week of the new camp, some ten thousand of the displaced people died of cholera alone. It spread rapidly through the camp and claimed the lives of more than thirty people per day. The funerals were held on a daily basis in Anakdiar. If you became sick in the morning, you died in the afternoon. We dug shallow graves in the ground with sticks to bury our loved ones and friends. It was a terrible time for us in the camp where you ate with your friend in the morning and buried him or her in the evening. Many displaced persons continued to die from cholera, dysentery, malaria and other preventable but life-threatening diseases. In fact, the risk of cholera stemmed from the use of unclean, muddy drinking water in Sobat River which was contaminated from the corpses polluting the river and from inadequate sanitation. These factors caused more than eighty percent of all diseases in the camp. The number claimed by cholera in Anakdiar Displaced Camp exceeded the number of the people who were killed by the Nuer militias. After the cholera outbreak, other diseases, such as whooping cough, chicken fox and typhoid fever, attacked the camp. I survived cholera in both Anakdiar and Renk Displaced Camp. After five months, the government broke up the camp and allowed everyone to go to their relatives in Malakal. I went to Malakal with my family and then proceeded to Renk to seek employment there. From Malakal on the 14th of September, 1992 we rode by river steamer to Renk. It took us four days to travel by sea from Malakal to Renk.

HEADING TO RENK IN SEARCH OF WORK

We got off the ship at Renk and were escorted to the displaced camp by the welcoming committee to the school building compound in Renk where hundreds of sleeping displaced persons were sheltered by the County authority. Many people lay sprawled across the school building and I was one of those. Others drifted to the sprawling cities, such as Renk, while the rest headed off to Kenana in Northern Sudan with the hope of finding work there. After nearly one month in the school compound, I employed on a durra plantation as a manual worker. This plantation was owned privately. After almost one month in the school compound, I moved my mother and siblings to the house that we were able to rent after I got work. Renk was the best place I had ever lived and I quickly adjusted to the hard work. I worked on a plantation eighty kilometres outside of Renk for six months. After this I lived in Renk for six months. This pattern of six months on and six months off continued for two years. In October 1992, cholera hit the displaced camp in Renk and claimed the lives of more than seventy people from Dinka Ngok Lual Yak, displaced persons who had survived the cholera that hit Anakdiar Displaced Camp in May of the same year.

I met my former girl friend better known by her nick name as Jongdit Rach in Renk in 1993 when I was living there with my mother and siblings. But her real name is withheld for her privacy. She was a luckless individual like me because her mother had died when she was still young and she was raised together with her younger sister by her strict single father while I was raised by a single mother. During the day I met Jongdit Rach, and then I invited her to come to my house later in the evening. In the first evening of our meeting, I asked her to be my girl friend. After lengthy words of introduction and so on, she agreed to my request and sat down next to me on the bare floor. This was the first time I had spent the whole night with a girl beside me. We joked and shared laughs together in the dark grass hut.

Chapter 11

THE PURSUIT OF SECONDARY SCHOOL

In 1994 I went to Wad-madeni in search of a high school education. Determined to make the goal of going back to school possible, I decided to go to school full time and get a full-time flexible job in order to support myself and my family. To earn my daily bread, I was working in a hotel as security guard at night and going to school during the day. I was treated like a dog by the Yugoslavian mischievous hotel owner Mr. Salah. He was the most obsessive and cruel businessman I have ever met in my life. I would take books to work and read them by the light of the moon in front of the hotel. Mr. Salah used me as a human fence to guard his property, including his cars. He would lock me outside the hotel in the rain to watch his cars. I would spend the nights hanging outside the hotel without bedding where I would look miserable as though I was waiting for someone to meet me until my boss would call me to get inside the building in the morning. The hotel owner used to order me to be killed first by thieves before they stole his cars. It was not a very pleasant job, but I kept it because it paid for school fees and living expenses for myself and for my family. My salary from this work was only six thousand Sudanese pounds per month (four dollars US). This was in 1995, at a time when breakfast and dinner could cost you nearly two thousand Sudanese pounds. But the good part was that I would eat once a day, something I was already accustomed to from living in the Ethiopian Refugee Camp. In spite of these situations, I was somehow able to graduate from high school with high marks. I did well with many subjects, except math and religion.

I resided in Wad-medani during the school year and went to Gaderef city in eastern Sudan during the school break in the summer to find employment at various simsim fields in the rural areas around Gederef city, a situation that supplied both food and board. Sometimes we faced the challenge of not getting employment which meant no food and board. On rare occasions, we slept on the floor in an empty place in an adjacent black area, where we tried not to be seen by passersby.

I took my youngest brother, Dhot Chol Lual to Medani to stay with me where I enrolled him in school. I was worried about his future because he was my only brother. The financial situation in Wad-medani was poor so I stopped taking the bus and I often walked to school. With the bus fare money saved, I was able to pay money for a hot drink for my younger brother Dhot and me at dinner times. I could afford one meal a day. In Wad-medani, we were living as teams of friends and room-mates who could share food quietly like twins. On the week-end, we would gather in one place and joke till the middle of the night, laughing heartily over something we were discussing. We would get more excited, particularly when Mr. Miyom Bol Nyok and Deng Mabil Awuol were there, because they were the amus-ing ones. I had been living with my friend Deng Mabil Awuol, who became like my blood brother. The teams of friends in-cluded Thon Mayiik Ding, as well as Deng Monybuny Kur and Gach Deng Bul who was about to marry at the time. In October 1995, I went to Gederaf with my friend Deng Mabil Awuol to cut simsim there. After our work Deng Mabil Awuol decided to go to Ethiopia to further his education there. I opted to remain in Sudan, partly to care for my aging mother and siblings who still heavily relied on me. We exchanged goodbyes with Deng Mabil Awuol, who left Sudan on 20 October, 1995 for Ethiopia via Asmara in Eritrea and lost contact until my arrival in Egypt nearly seven years later.

After saying farewell to Deng Mabil Awuol, I worked in the simsim field for a few days. There were scorpions and snakes in the field and I was stung in the middle of the night by a scorpi-on. The powerful pain from the scorpion sting was as painful as that of snakes. I endured the scorpion sting for the whole night without help. The next morning I decided to go to Gederaf and then proceeded to Wad-medani, rather than stay in the simsim field with some mistrusted men who had plotted to rob me and run away with my money. I told these suspicious men that I was going to fetch some drinking water in the nearby river and they agreed. After that, I hurriedly crossed the river and took a ride in a truck to Gedaref city. After two days in Gedaref, it turned out the same men had followed me when I accidentally met one of these men in the Gederaf market. He was a little drunk so he assured me that they were planning to rob me after sunset on the day I had escaped. I looked frankly into his eyes and he looked like a half-drowned rat as he walked along the road.

After four days in Gedaref, I went to Wadmedani and spent some time there before moving to Kenana to look for a job. In my final high school year in 1995, my late half brother Kon Mamor Lual began to consult me about the possibility of my going to the Bible College in Malakal. I laughed at the thought, saying that you would not catch me in a place like that. I was not an active member in the church and I never went to church every Sunday as I do with my family now. My childhood dream after I went to school was to be a lawyer and I had no intention of being a missionary. Furthermore, the idea of spending a life time serving God in a traditional dominated society like Ajuba where my mother was still practicing her traditional beliefs was too awesome for me. In addition, milking cows in Ajuba rural community had persuaded me that theological seminary was not my calling and instead I went to Wad-madeni Secretarial Institute to study management for eight months. This course equipped me with the administrative skills I have continued to develop. After I received a diploma in administration, I devoted the next three years to my family which included my mother and siblings.

WORKING IN KENANA SUGAR COMPANY

I went to Kenana on the 31st of October, 1995 to look for work. I needed to get immediate employment to support my elderly mother and siblings. I stayed in Kenana for two weeks and on the 15th of November I got a job there with Kenana Sugar Company Limited (KSC). As a manual worker I worked hard to look after my elderly mother and siblings, making sure that there was a roof over their heads. During summers much seasonal labour from Southern Sudan used to migrate to northern Sudan where most of these labourers worked in Kenana as menial labourers. When I graduated in the college with a diploma in administration, I made it my personal priority to get married in 1996. When I revealed this idea to my long-time girl friend Jongdit Rach she was too shy about my marriage proposal and brought pointless excuses about her reluctance to become a wife in that year. In the summer of 1996, I left Kenana for Renk to discuss this issue with my former girl friend. After nearly two nights in conversation, nothing was fruitful from this subject. She refused my proposal for the time being. I spent two sleepless nights without any agreement, plus she wanted more time to consider the proposal. In the early morning she asked whether she could come back later in the evening to discuss this marriage proposal once again. Finally I told her to forget this worthless friendship with me and I returned to Kenana with my mother to resume work after my vacation. After I left school, I decided to let my younger brother Dhot to concentrate his studies instead and focus on my responsibility to the family. My brother Dhot was in elementary school. However, I chose to get married as a relief to my mother who also yearned to see me with a family of my own. After I got employment in Kenana, I told my mother about my idea to get married. She agreed without any hesitation. Then I set about fulfilling a dream of having my own big family. The death of my own father had truly left me like a wingless bird on the earth. I had neither father nor a paternal uncle whom I could consult for support and advice in my life. I felt the absence of the above mentioned relatives during my marriage in 1996.

I finally got married on the 2nd of June, 1996 in Kenana where my wife Aluel Deng Nyok was living with her parents. My traditional wedding ceremony was supposed to be attended by my uncles as was the custom in Dinka society. Instead, my mother was the one who represented me in my own marriage to fill the shoes of my late father Chol Lual Kiir and my uncles. On the other hand, there was no representation from my maternal relations in my wedding ceremony due to the severe envy of my so-called maternal uncle Thuc Ayuel Koryom whom my mother insisted on identifying as her half brother. My maternal uncle Thuc Ayuel Koryom was invited in advance to attend my wedding ceremony where he would rightfully represent me as my maternal uncle, but he did not attend for unknown reasons, nor his two sons. I wished my maternal grandmother Arop Monyjok Reth and my maternal aunt Akon Ayuel Koryom were alive to help my mother in my marriage ceremony. Despite all these matters and envy, my mother managed to settle everything and I welcomed my wife Aluel Deng Nyok into my own house in the evening of June 2nd, 1996.

I got the love of my life and I shook her hand before the fifteen people, mostly friends and relatives who attended her reception to my house in that evening. The handshake in front of family meant that all the agreements between the families are finalized and the groom welcomes his wife into his home by shaking her hand in front of family. She has now been publicly welcomed into the groom's home. They are married.

I am still quite sure that when my younger brother Dhot Chol Lual marries, he will face the same lack of representation from our maternal relations, let alone those of our paternal relations who are just selfish who "want something to eat from us, not something to serve." That expression means that they would be willing to receive the cows from a marriage agreement but they would not be willing to provide the cows. Traditionally uncles and brothers can contribute cows towards the bride price and then they can also expect to receive cows when a girl in the family is married. These male relatives had received gladly the cows from my sister's marriage but were unwilling to contribute towards the bride price for my marriage.

Despite the lack of support from some family members, we enjoyed our young family life together as husband and wife until misfortune hit us in the chest. On the 6th of December 1996, we lost our first male child who died in childbirth. The infant corpse was buried by my mother with my cousin Magong Dhieu Kiir. It was really horrible for my wife and me to watch the burial of our first-born baby. However, this was the start of our mourning and we endured this loss for a long while. One year later, our second child Kiir was born in November, 1997 in Kenana and I became a father for the first time. Kiir sometimes would crawl briefly to play on the grave of our first-born child, and it would remind me of my son. I would try to encourage Kiir not to play on this place of respect.

The love of a parent is perpetual and endless. It is also inspirational as I still feel the love that my mother has given us, but I think I understood it more when I became a parent myself on the day my son Kiir was born. After two years, our third child, Lual was born in February 2000 in Kenana. Our children were named after the family names that were mostly chosen by my mother and the relatives. We were still hoping to have at least one daughter, but such was not to be at the desired time. In November 2007, my wife and I had a daughter and my sons finally got the sister they were yearning for. My daughter Arop was born on the 28th November, 2007 in Canada after nearly eight years without a baby. Shortly after the birth of my daughter Arop, I was able to hold her for the first time. After that, I took the chance to announce the arrival of our daughter to my sons who were overjoyed to welcome her into our family. My mother Nyanbuny Ayuel Koryom was delighted in Sudan about the birth of Arop for good reason. She had been praying for us to have a baby girl since our marriage. The baby was named Arop in memory of her late mother Arop Monyjok Reth. My mother Nyanbuny Ayuel was so happy and proud for the honour given to her late mother.

FACING NEPOTISM IN KENANA

In 1998, I had been looking for a job and I applied for the job of scrap that was assigned to the weary Southerners in Kenana to do because it was one of the dirty jobs. Scrap means picking up the small pieces of sugar cane left in the harvesting process. The work crew was run by two self-interested individuals as foremen from the Ngok Lual Yak clan under the leadership of a drunken Arab man named Assam. I thought that the work would be open to everybody, including me, but this was not to be the case. I applied through my former employer, Abdalaziz Mohamed. The job was a new opening and the foremen's first priority was to employ their relatives and in-laws. Since the leaders in question were single themselves, their second priority was to employ girls and young married women with a secret scheme to use them later as their concubines or girl friends. My initial plan was to work as a labourer with no intention of seeking the position of controller. But when I approached Assam, the Manager of the scrap, for the job with my former employer, Abdalaziz who was his fellow Arab Muslim, Assam transferred me to the then foreman Kuol Deng Chan to recruit me as a labourer who would only clean the dirty cane in the field. But there was a fixed mandate for employment. First you must be either from Dhiak section if you wanted to work with Kuol Deng Chan or originally from Awier section if you wanted to work with Akoc Dupel. If you failed to meet these criteria, then you must have connections through marriage or other relatives to support your application for employment. These individuals definitely practiced nepotism. This was my first time to meet with Kuol Deng Chan and I thought that I would get the job but he did not know me and I did not know him. In addition, I was accused by one of his employee from Ngar section, a former acquaintance of mine, that I was a radical man who would seize his position as soon as I was employed in his department because this employee was concerned about my good handwriting and knowledge of English. At that time no one there could write a good report in English even though all the paper work and report writing of the Kenana Sugar Company was supposed to be done in English. Secondly, these individuals presumed my Arab friend Abdalaziz had links with the security services. They accused me of plotting to take over the leadership of Kuol Deng Chan and Mr. Kuol Deng Chan himself believed them. These accusations against me to usurp their jobs were groundless. As a result, the position I applied for was left vacant for almost two months until one of his close relatives from Dhiak section come along from Ngok to occupy it.

I thought I was close to those of Dhiak section because I have many in-laws there from the side of my half brother Dhieu Kiir Lual and Dol Kiir Lual who both were married in Dhiak section so I thought I would have been treated with dignity. In addition, my half sister Achol Kiir Lual was married in Dhiak section to Chol Jang, but it seemed that all these links were not helpful. In Awier section itself; I have a very strong connection because my late maternal aunt Akon Ayuel Koryom was married there. But all these links did not bring relief or persuade these men to hire me in the scrap department.

It was obvious that our people were still practicing nepotism in Northern Sudan where they were used to employing their own relatives and close friends while those who have no family links to them were excluded. Somehow I managed to get employment elsewhere in Kenana without facing further nepotism.

I thought I might have left this nepotism behind in Sudan after I came to Egypt in 2002 with my family. Little did I know that I might face the same issues in Egypt. As one of the members of the Dinka Ngok Lual Yak community, our names were sent to Australia for possible sponsorship application forms. To my surprise, my name was erased in Australia for the reason that I was not wanted there by one of the Ngok fellows who had been kicked out of his house several times in Australia by his own wife due to his deceitfulness. After my brother in-law Guil Amol Guil went to Australia, he sent me an application form right away and I thanked him for his loyalty to the entire community of Dinka Ngok Lual Yak, regardless of its eleven sections. He treated me and my family with dignity as he had covered the gap of being denied an application form for Australia by one of the recognized fellow from Ngok Lual Yak clan. Soon after I submitted my application form to the Australian Consulate in Egypt, I was recognized by the United Nations High Commissioner for Refugees in Cairo, Egypt for resettlement in Canada with my family. After two months, my file was transferred to the Canadian Consulate in Cairo. I was able to leave Egypt for Canada within seventeen months of my stay in Egypt, making me one of the blessed people who left Egypt without having to stay longer.

Chagai Chol Lual

Chapter 12

THE YEARS OF BEREAVEMENT AND DEPRESSION

In 1998 we suffered the grievous loss of our brother Kon Mamor Lual who died in Khartoum after a long illness. My half-brother Kon Mamor Lual was a man whose great compassion made him an object of love and respect in our family and beyond. For three years, he had been battling for peace among Dinka and Nuer who were torn apart by the split in Upper Nile State since 1992. Later, he grappled with pain and illness that eventually claimed his life. He liked everyone and everyone liked him. My half brother Kon Mamor Lual always extended his helping hand to anyone who asked for it, expecting nothing in return. He smiled even as he was suffered the exhaustion of a debilitating illness, sparing relatives the possible distress of pain. Anyone who met him assumed that he was living a life of perfect delight. Being a peace maker, it was his inner peace that radiated among the community during the major split in the SPLM/A movement. He never gave any sign of the severe sorrows he experienced, but rather spread love and unity among those who were around him. The smile never left his face until the last moment of his life. In addition to all these qualities, my half-brother Kon Mamor Lual was extremely caring since he knew how to disarm people, extracting the best from them while neutralizing tensions in our community. The death of my half brother Kon Mamor Lual was a big blow to our relatives, and it was a great advantage to his political enemies in Baliet County who were celebrating his death while our relatives and the entire Ajuba community were mourning his death.

After the death of my half brother Kon Mamor Lual, then my half brother Tor Wuor Lual died in 2000 in Kenana after four years of battling illness. The paternal relations of Kiir Arieu were shocked by the death of our beloved brothers. Later, my half brother Chuang Ayom Lual, who was in charge of our family spirits, as he used to declare himself, was in extreme stress and in a bad mood after the death of our beloved relatives. He stopped his constant laughter and soon seemed to be desperate. Not only was my brother in charge of our family spirits, he was also claiming to be a spear master, a right he had borrowed from his maternal relations because we have no such things like a spear master in the history of Kiir Arieu family. Shortly afterward he became sick, probably due to the extreme stress he had gone through after the deaths of the above-mentioned brothers. He was lying on a mat on the bare floor, pale and frail, so I took him to the hospital in Kenana where he was admitted for one week, but he requested to be removed from the hospital to die in the hands of his relatives which he did. I would glance at my beloved half brother Chuang Ayom Lual as he was lying hopeless in my house, and I was doubtful about why even an important person who used to be a soothsayer and prayed to his family spirits frequently had to endure such misery. I often look after my half brother Chuang Ayom Lual throughout his illness in Kenana and it was an opportunity to care for him to the end of his life. My brother Chuang Ayom Lual would often get restless if I was not sitting and speaking with him. He died quietly in my arms in Kenana in 2001 at the age of fifty-four. Only a few weeks before his death, I had spent a wonderful evening together with him after my wife Aluel Deng Nyok had made a traditional home made wine in his honour. After he had sipped the traditional Dinka homemade wine, he started to sing his own songs loudly in Dinka and then he stood up and danced like a young man. A few weeks before his illness, he often had to deal with his heavy drinking after his wife and three children had died and it seemed that God had turned against him. He had five children and two of them had grown to adulthood while the rest had passed away.

The deaths of those brothers were a great loss for the families of Lual Kiir Arieu and for me personally because, in every respect, they were wonderful brothers to me and I especially missed them at large family gatherings. For me, these were some of the hardest years of my life. After all these losses, I was able to send this heart-breaking news to our relatives in Baliet County in Southern Sudan where most of my relatives were staying. There was no telephone communication so the news was passed by word of mouth. Our relatives were shocked and the families were in grief from 1998 to 2001.

Finally we thought that death may have taken a break. However, we were again shocked by the sudden death of my half brother Monyjok Kiir Deng in Kenana. After he fell sick in the middle of the night, he was rushed to the hospital in Kenana but he died before he reached the hospital. I was away at work during his sudden death, but I came home the next day. Shortly after my arrival, my half-sister Nyankuany Miyom Lual told me that our brother Monyjok Kiir Deng had suffered a massive heart attack earlier that evening and was dead. I almost fainted and sobbed when I heard of the untimely death of our brother. I had left him as a healthy man who was full of life with a big smile in his face.

My half brother Monyjok Kiir Deng was single and he had left no instructions about his will nor how he would be represented during his absence. I managed to obtain his death certificate from the Municipal in Kenana after a long process and we were able to collect his pensions from the Kenana Sugar Company. The initial partial compensation of the late Monyjok Kiir Deng was squandered by cheaters and nephews due to the timidity of my cousin Kiir Ayiei Kiir to whom we had assigned the responsibility of the funds, according to the family line. Finally, after the life insurance money was received I was able to call the family meeting to discuss the way that the money of the deceased would be spent with my three cousins, Magong Dhieu Kiir, Agok Wieu Miyom and Kiir Ayiei Kiir. We resolved that the funds would be used to arrange the marriage of a woman with the deceased. This custom is known as ghost marriage in the Dinka traditions to ensure offspring for the family of the late Monyjok Kiir Deng. I moved that the money of the deceased would be given to my Cousin Kiir Ayiei Kiir in order to marry the wife of his paternal uncle Monyjok Kiir, according to the family arrangement. In a few months, I sped up the process and my cousin Kiir Ayiei Kiir got married then and the family of the late Monyjok Kiir Deng was represented as requested. Once more, my relatives at home thanked me heartily for the part I had played in making this marriage successful, and I sincerely thanked my cousins for their understanding and cooperation. The family of our late brother Monyjok Kiir Deng is now fully represented by my cousin Kiir Ayiei Kiir who has currently fathered three children from that marriage which I coordinated as his uncle while I was still in Sudan. Additionally, it was one of my personal responsibilities towards my own relatives. In Dinka society where we belong a person must achieve the goals that please the entire relatives, otherwise you may be called a heartless individual by the relatives.

JOURNEY FULL OF DETOURS AND TERRIBLE HARDSHIPS

In May 2000 I decided to leave Sudan for Egypt. My decision to leave my mother was not because I had given up my responsibility. When I told this idea to my mother, she became enraged and refused to listen to my idea. She had advised me to continue my education in Sudan and not to go abroad. My mother told me that we are living in a time of war and scattering places. She also told me that my siblings wanted me to be around to see them and besides she was getting old. It broke my heart and I told my mother that I knew she was old and my siblings wanted me to be with them. Since I was the obedient son to my mother I resolved to stay but still held a hope that God would change her heart. Because the Dinka culture values family thus the eldest son is expected to take care of his aging parents and live with them even after marriage.

In 2001 my mother gladly told me that she had agreed to let me to go to Egypt. She supported my decision because Sudan was not a safe place for young people like me to live in due to the insecurity in the entire nation. The successive regimes in Khartoum had been drawing the youth and young men into a fighting force on religious grounds, terming the armed struggle in the South as enemies of Islam. This had happened during the civil war where the regimes in the north advocated for the total destruction of the non-Arabs and non-Muslims from Sudan, but the authorities were still pursuing youth and young men for military service. They were able to trail Southern Sudanese into their villages and jungles for taking up arms to fight for their dignity.

Before I left Sudan, my mother instructed me to not forget her and my siblings whom she said relied on me as the eldest brother in our family. In February 2001 I moved from Kenana to Khartoum to get the documents for my emigration to Egypt. Once I arrived in Khartoum, my half brother Ranlei Abiel Lual misled me that his best friend Miyom from Dinka Bor was a broker for entry visas. He strongly advised me to let Miyom obtain my entry visa from the Egyptian Consulate in Khartoum. Being trustful of my half brother Ranlei Abiel Lual, whom I thought would not befriend a thief, I handed my passport and two hundred Sudanese pounds to Miyom to obtain my entry visa from the Egyptian Consulate in Khartoum. After three days I learned this man had taken my money and disappeared with my passport in Khartoum. I tried to locate this heartless thief for nearly six days. I was often hungry and thirsty because there was no food or water due to the Muslim Holy month of Ramadan in the entire country where Arabs were dominating everything. I suddenly caught him red-handed amongst his friends from the Dinka Bor Community and gave him a look of horror. He looked like an honest man as he tried to smile to wash away his shameful disappearance with my passport. I resisted sharing a laugh with him that he thought would calm me down. I told Miyom that if the entire Dinka Bor Community were deceitful like you, nobody would have bothered to follow you to the bush. These words raised many eyebrows amongst the Dinka Bor community members who were around during my tirade. Later one of the Dinka Bor police majors grabbed my left arm ruthlessly and took me together with Miyom to the place where Miyom had hidden my passport. He handed it to me with teary eyes. In my own eyes I was actually an innocent person and a victim of fraud, but the police major was angry with me for the serious insults I used against his fellow brother. He was looking for a way to imprison me but there was nothing wrong that he could claim to charge me for. After I said these words I realized I was out of line to annoy the entire Bor community and I made an apology.

I thought that my half brother Ranlei Abiel Lual was a man with dignity who could never do this to his half brother but it seemed to me that my half brother Ranlei had adopted the life of city people who never cared about their shameful tricking of their own relatives who came from the remote areas where fraud is very rare. It was a mistake and I will never trust him again.

After all these obstacles, I was able to obtain the entry visa for Egypt from the Egyptian consulate in Khartoum. I obtained all the necessary papers, including the exit visa from the Ministry of Interior Affairs in Khartoum. Afterwards I went back to Kenana to collect my children and my wife so that we could leave together for Egypt. Upon my arrival in Kenana, my elder sister Areng Chol Lual sent me an urgent letter from Renk urging me to come to Renk to attend to her husband who was extremely sick with diarrhea. My sister insisted that I be present in Renk because she had just delivered a baby while her husband was hospitalized. She was caring for her infant and a sick husband. It was an appalling situation that required much support from my side and I did my part to relieve my elder sister. This was on March 4, 2001. On the one hand I had the entry visas to go to Egypt with my family with all expenses paid for, but on the other hand, I also wanted to take care of my siblings and my mother. This was my first test and my heart was divided first about what to do. I wanted to go to Egypt as planned and I did not want to disappoint my elder sister, so being the elder son in our family made me put the needs of my siblings before my own because the responsibility of our family was on my shoulders as it was and still is. So I accepted her request because there was no one else and the need was undeniable. I cancelled my journey, much to the astonishment of the neighbors and friends and I went to Renk to attend the ailing husband of my sister. I knew that it was the right choice for me to give up my own emigration process to Egypt for the sake of my elder sister, even though that process cost me hundreds of thousands pounds for my tickets and the other paper work which I have paid for earlier. My wife Aluel, who is one of the same cultural backgrounds, initially agreed to this living arrangement and allowed me to fulfill my duty as the elder son.

I left my wife and children in Kenana and headed to Renk to be with my elder sister during this difficult time. Upon my arrival in Renk on the 6th of March 2001, I found the husband of my sister was awake but he was entirely helpless. In fact, his condition was critical and the doctor had given up all hope. Four days later he was dead, leaving my sister behind with four children, including her two-week-old son named Dhieu. I left for Melut immediately after the funeral to see my cousin Kuol Chuang Ayom. Additionally, I was not aware that I would face unexpected hardship there in Melut where I have trusted friends and cousin.

MY FRUITLESS TRIP TO MELUT IN 2001

After spending a week in Renk, I made my way to Melut to visit my cousin Kuol Chuang Ayom and my best friend Chigai Ajang Deng who were in the Sudan Armed Force based in Melut County which is an oil-rich county in Upper Nile State. Melut was crowded by the Arab security elements due to the war at that time between the ruling regime in Khartoum and the Sudan People Liberation Army (SPLA). I reached Melut after a journey by truck of almost eight thousand miles. The road was a sand track full of bumps and hollows, but it was still one of the better routes in a sprawling country of poverty and conflict. I arrived safely in Melut later in the evening. I was only going to be there for about one week because I was on my way to Kenana. After I briefed my cousin Kuol Chuang Ayom about the wills of his late father Chuang Ayom Lual who had died earlier in Kenana, I then went to the house of my friend Chigai Ajang Deng who lived close to the Sudanese army of Melut. I stayed in the house of my friend Chigai Ajang Deng in Melut. He accommodated me as his special friend in his home and I slept in one of his houses.

I had met Chigai Ajang Deng in Renk in 1993 and soon we became close friends. We were full of youthful passion and had a lot of strength. At first this visit gave nothing but joy to my friend Chigai Ajang Deng who begged his wife Achol Kuel to give me her particular care and attention. Moreover, he seemed to be quite cheerful when he was with his old friend. We talked about the old times and we remembered our school days as well as our early youth together in Renk. We started our joking from the lessons that we had learned in the school and ended our jokes with the memories of our former girl friends in early 1993 before each of us were married and had fathered a child. He told the history of our youth to his wife Achol Kuel, who constantly took a cheerful part in those conversations. His wife Achol begged me to make my stay longer. This generous woman prepared all kinds of food for me and I ate everything from cocks to beef. Fish was on the menu regularly, as well as the coffee which was the favorite hot drink in the life of Melut residents. In the evening of my arrival, the first dinner was a meal of traditional food and cock that were eaten while we were sitting cross-legged on the mat brought by Achol Kuel. I was glad to share the food with my friend Chigai Ajang and my cousin Kuol Chuang Ayom for the first time in three years. It was a great experience to share the stories from Renk while we were eating the traditional food in the bright atmosphere. It was the first festival that I had ever had in my honour and I deeply enjoyed it. We discussed family matters with my cousin Kuol. Afterward I told him and my friend Chigai that I did not have enough funds for my trip back to Renk. They both gave me the impression that I would be looked after in Melut and that they would take care of my transport expenses back to Renk, but things turned out otherwise.

My cousin Kuol made me promise to wait for him until he received his salary so that he could give me some funds for my transport back to Renk. Then he went to the army barrack in Melut, telling me that he would get back to me within two days. However, I waited long-sufferingly for my cousin for three weeks, but he failed to turn up. I learned afterward that my cousin had received his salary previously. Instead of coming back to let me know that he had changed his mind, he simply stayed in the army barracks, pretending that he was still waiting for his so called salary. My cousin Kuol Chuang Ayom had been drinking heavily before, and I had advised him previously to quit his heavy drinking, but the death of his father encouraged him to run back to the bottle and succumb to lying. Now I was waiting for him to return, wasting valuable days in a tight security war zone in Melut area. I was fully confident that my cousin Kuol Chuang Ayom would not do something like that, because I believed he would tell me clearly if he was not going to come and would not leave me in suspense, exposed to unnecessary risks. My close friend Mr. Chigai Ajang Deng, who had promised to do me something earlier also, did not live up to his promise and he did not show up either.

I had never been in Melut and I was not prepared for the obstacle course I would go through there. At that time I contracted diarrhea that almost killed me in rural Melut where medicines were rare. I spent the most miserable two weeks of my life outside in the cold nights due to the diarrhea. I thank God that I was saved from the Sudan Armed Forces who used to patrol the area at night. My cousin Kuol Chuang Ayom stayed in the army barrack and it was clear that he was not bothered about my health situation. I tried numerous attempts to reach my friend Chigai Ajang Deng by sending his own wife Achol Kuel to him in the army barracks with my letter that I had written, but he did not show up. Even though I was in his house as a special guest and his personal best friend, he simply ended up in the army barrack as well as my cousin Kuol until the day I boarded the steamer boat to Renk. His wife Achol Kuel was the one who bade me farewell instead.

APPALLING EXPERIENCE IN MELUT TOWN

This experience was shocking, to say the least, especially being disappointed by these individuals. Having waited in vain for three weeks for my cousin to return, I began to feel this was pointless and was turning into a wasted trip. I sat in the shade under a tree, feeling a little sorry for myself. I grabbed a pen and wrote my application to the deputy Commissioner of Melut County to ask for financial assistance in the form of cash to cover my transport expenses back to Renk. Sitting behind an impressive desk, the deputy commissioner asked me to be seated. The old man appeared to be comfortable in his lightly grass-thatched office in the war-torn area. I gave him my letter but he asked me about the purpose of my visit before he even read my letter. After I told him about my visit, then he stiffened and gave me a long hard look through his thick eye glasses. After he had read my letter he relaxed in his makeshift woody arm chair. To my delight the Deputy Commissioner approved my request without question and authorized his corrupt cashier (who would cheat me later) to give me the sum of fifty thousand Sudanese pounds without further delay. Should the deputy commissioner have attempted to ask me more questions about my work in addition to the place where I came from, I could simply tell him that I was a student from the University of Juba and I had come from Khartoum to visit my cousin Kuol Chuang Ayom whom I found out that he had been transferred to the Maban garrison. But my good handwriting had his attention, so he did not bother to request further information from me other than my identity card. I left his office deeply grateful for his kindness and rushed to the office of the cashier with the hope that I would receive the amount that his boss had approved for me. To my surprise, the corrupt Shilluk cashier deducted thirty thousand Sudanese pounds for some anonymous reason and gave me twenty thousand Sudanese pounds instead, shouting loudly that the money he had in his cash box was supposed to be given to disabled persons and powerless residents of Melut. Due to my desperate need, I received the twenty thousand Sudanese pounds in silence and started grumbling. At 3:30 p.m. I took the river streamer to Renk and arrived there after a one-night journey.

In reality, if my cousin Kuol Chuang Ayom had not been there in Melut as part of his military duty, I would not have visited Melut. But I went to Melut to brief him about the instructions of the will that his late father Chuang Ayom Lual had left me to be passed on to his son Kuol following his death in 2001. At the time of the death of my half brother Chuang Ayom Lual, his son Kuol was in Melut garrison where he was serving as a soldier in the Sudan Armed Force. When I visited Melut, I hoped I would get support from my cousin Kuol Chuang Ayom and my friend Chigai Ajang Deng. Instead I finally returned to Renk with nothing more than frustration from the visit. I returned empty-handed and traveled with Gieth Wuor Mabok from Melut by river streamer to Renk. Upon my arrival in Renk, I proceeded to the Catholic High School in Renk to see my best friend Mr. Chigai Miyom Wuor, after I briefly met my sister Areng Chol Lual with her children. As soon as my friend Chigai Miyom Wuor saw me, he was seemed confused and said he did not believe that I was still in Melut. My friend Chigai Miyom Wuor presumed I had gone straight to Kenana without a stopover in Renk. We dawdled over coffee and I related to him the situation that I went through in Melut before we turned our focus on my emigration process for Egypt, a program to which he had contributed earlier. After four days in Renk, I took my sister with her children to Kenana where my family was living in order to discuss their future with my mother. In June 2001, my mother resolved that she go with her two daughters Nyanyiik and Areng and her grandchildren to Baliet town in the Upper Nile State of Southern Sudan to stay with my half brother Dol Kiir Lual and the relatives who lived there.

Chagai Chol Lual

Chapter 13

BACK TO BALIET COUNTY AND BACK TO FARMING

When we fled from Ngok Lual Yak land to Northern Sudan we were among the thousands of Ngok Lual Yak people who believed that we would be back in the area within a matter of months, but we would spend nearly six years away from home in the grass-thatched huts in Kenana. On June 10, 2001, I took my mother, my sister Nyanyiik and my elder sister Areng with her children from Kenana to Baliet via Malakal as requested by my mother. At this time I left my wife Aluel and my two beloved sons Kiir and Lual in Kenana, and I promised them that I would be back after one month, but the resettlement of my mother, my sisters and my nephews in Baliet took me four more months instead because I farmed a field for them.

We arrived in Malakal during the heavy rains and proceeded to the house of my late half brother Kon Mamor Lual where we met a few relatives who were residing in Malakal, including my half brother Monytong Wuor Lual who was not aware of our coming back. When we arrived in Malakal with my cousin Kiir Ayiei Kiir, our relatives were very happy to meet us. After one hour of reunion, my half brother Monytong Wuor Lual joked when he was asked why he did not go to the port when he had seen the ship coming from northern Sudan. He answered that he did not bother to go because no relatives in the north ever returned. Most of our relatives, friends and neighbors shared this assumption. The example was my half brother, the late Monyjok Kiir Deng, who went to the north and spent more than thirty years there in Northern Sudan until he died in Kenana in Northern Sudan without getting married. Moreover, my half brother Riak Mamor Lual who went to Northern Sudan in 1969 had never return nor married nor given back to the relatives as requested. I had the privilege of meeting him in 1998 in Kenana. He was toothless and without any dream of marriage as expected by Dinka norms. When I tried to challenge him to either get married or to support the children of his late brother Kon Mamor Lual, he just nodded his head and smiled, baring his missing teeth. The relatives took his marriage as a priority and urged him to marry. My half-brother Riak Mamor Lual was not very pleased with all these suggestions which he thought would limit his regular drinking. Afterward, my half brother Riak Mamor Lual escaped to a remote area of Northern Sudan, and I did not meet him again until my departure to Egypt. All these things made my relatives more cautious toward family members who did not return after many years in exile.

After my arrival in Baliet area in 2001 with my mother and siblings, I was able to meet my friends there and I even had the opportunity to move to Wune Ding village and to my home village of Ayok Lual Kiir in Ajuba district purposely for a short trip. I met with my relatives plus others who were living in my home area before. It was a very great joy for me to see my homeland for the second time after eight more years in Northern Sudan. After nearly three months in Ngok land, I returned to Kenana to see my family. On October 29, 2001, I arrived in Kenana and rejoined my wife Aluel Deng Nyok and children. However, I spent three more months in Kenana with my family before I resumed my emigration process.

UNEXPECTEDLY HOMELESS IN KENANA IN 2002

Shortly before leaving for Egypt, I went through another bout of testing after I left Kenana for Khartoum on January 26, 2002 to revive the emigration process that I had postponed previously. I obtained the entry visa on January 28, 2002 in the Egyptian Consulate in Khartoum. The next day I returned to Kenana to collect my wife and children so that we could leave together for Egypt. I took the bus from Khartoum to Kenana and once I got off at the bus station, I met the homeless man who said he hadn't eaten in a few days. Instead of ignoring him, I took him over to the nearby restaurant and I ordered him the food he desperately requires. At that instant I looked up at him and saw that he had tears in his eyes. He told me that nobody had ever been so kind to him. He got his food and I wished him good luck. I left him sitting in the restaurant and asked me to pray for him and his homeless friends. I prayed for the homeless people yet I was not aware that I was praying for myself and my family. After this, I immediately went to the house of Duot Amol Mading to celebrate. I thought to myself that all my problems were finally over, but I did not know that they were just beginning. After a cup of coffee, I told Duot Amol Mading, about the idea of my leaving for Egypt. He was pleased and wished me success. It was Wednesday afternoon when I had coffee with Duot and others.

Soon my cousin Dhal Dol Kiir, whom I had left in my house with my family in Kenana earlier, came to the house of Duot Amol Mading After a brief chat with Duot Amol Mading over coffee, my cousin Dhal told me that someone had set my house on fire two days ago. Nothing had been saved in the house, except my wife and children. I thanked God for the safety of my family although the news alarmed me so I went to my family. When I got there I realized I had no house to go to because it had been burned to the ground. On reaching the compound, I did not look first at the ash of my burned house because my eyes were glued to my children and my wife. Finally it upset me to glance at the pitiful ruins of black ash of our family house that had been devastated by fire. My wife was standing sad and gloomy, but I exhorted her to not worry and to persist in praying to God through this test. My family was without a roof over their heads for almost two days before the community built them a shelter during my absence. Later my wife and children were sheltered in a small thatched grass hut that the community built after the fire. The fire devastated our house and left my family with almost nothing except the clothes they wore. As I saw my family in such a state, my eyes filled with tears and I called out my older son Kiir. He ran to me and jumped into my arms. He said, "You won't go away again father, will you?" Those were his first words to me and I will never forget them as long as I live. Thank God, we were both strong in our trust and loyalty to each other through the situation we were facing. We slept in that grass hut which had been built by the neighbours.

It was the neighbours who helped my family rebuild their home and lives after the fire. This was a simple thing for neighbours to be helping neighbours. Some of my close relatives, including my cousins were there in Kenana, but they did not bother to show up to visit my desperate family while I was still in Khartoum. This made me uncertain toward my own relatives, some of whom may have married in Kenana through my tireless efforts. Yet they did not care for my family during my absence. After the horrible fire, our neighbours were most caring and gave my family so many things, including cups and dishes. While we were low on food, a neighbor kindly brought us some traditional food. There were many holes in the roof of the hut but we just needed a roof over our heads, not a good hut. There was no rain, just extreme cold. It was freezing cold with many holes in the roof of the hut and the biting wind cut through our thin clothing. Life can be difficult at times but no human life is without its challenges. My children still recall that rough thatched grass hut we slept in. Imagine how a caring father feels when seeing his half naked children suffer from cold.

I wondered if this sort of testing might foil our planned journey to Egypt. Such thoughts were fleeting and I did not give them much time in my mind. I resisted the temptation to try other means. I thought generally to go to Khartoum and I was supported financially by my close friends Chigai Miyom Wuor and Ahol Awan Arop. These two friends of mine were with me in Ethiopia and they had experienced hardship in the past in the refugee camp. They were more generous towards me than some of my own relatives. It was my privilege to have a few true friends who cared about me. Mr. Chigai Miyom Wuor and Ahol Awan Arop, in particular, played a vital role in my journey to Egypt. We knew each other since our early childhood because they were from my original clan of cattle keepers and farmers. Mr. Chigai Miyom Wuor, in particular, had been a close friend of mine since our school days at Itang Refugee Camp in early 1989 in Ethiopia. He was slightly older than me and had been behind me at school, but he was a man who helped people without hesitation. We had been together for many years and were entirely comfortable with each other. In addition, the rare dinners we used to share in the refugee camp in Ethiopia drew us together. We remained devoted friends. Mr. Ahol Awan Arop was a man I had known since our early childhood in my home area of Ajuba where we all belonged. He was a good speaker, like his late father Awan Arop Mijok, though he is illiterate. We became good friends during his first marriage in 1995, because his relatives were of little support to him, but I supported him to the point where everything went well and he enjoyed this relationship with his wife Abuba Awan Achiek and the birth of a daughter. But unfortunately, his wife was unfaithful, and she was ultimately caught red-handed with another man. After their divorce, he was desperate and hopeless about his future. However, I was able to comfort this skinny man to forget everything that he had endured from his cheating wife and focus on his goal to remarry. I was committed to supporting him to get back on his feet by having a family of his own with the hope that his new family would bring him hope and happiness. Once again, I had a privilege of participating in his second wedding ceremony while I was still in Sudan in 2002 and I even sent him some money from Canada as part of my own contribution toward his marriage. Mr. Chigai Miyom Wuor and Ahol Awan Arop have survived the war atrocities in Sudan, and they are currently living in Southern Sudan with their families.

We had to leave Kenana in the winter, our only clothes being those we had on our backs. We held a farewell prayer service which was blessed by God. We left Kenana on February 12, 2002 by bus and arrived in Khartoum after a five-hour ride. We were accompanied to the bus station by my best friend Mr. Chigai Miyom Wuor, who was actually extremely concerned about my situation.

RESISTING TEMPTATIONS IN MY JOURNEY

When I arrived in Khartoum, I stayed in the house of Abraham Nyok Aguek during the time of my emigration process to go to Egypt. On February 13, I obtained our exit visa for Egypt and I got the exemption certificate from the office of the popular defense force in Khartoum. On February 17, I bought the tickets for both train and streamer. After I had completed all the necessary processes in Khartoum, however, I confirmed that the money which we had saved for our travel was now not enough to cover the rest of our next process. The sum of only fifty thousand Sudanese pounds was desperately needed by us to cover the exit fees in the Wadi-Halfa port. I appealed for help to the local Ngok Lual Yak community in Khartoum, including the businessman Abraham Nyok Aguek, because I thought that people would open their hearts and wallets to help me, but nobody seemed to have any interest in helping me and my family. Instead people just laughed and treated my situation as something of a joke. I had no choice but to cancel our trip that could have taken place the following Monday.

The matter of these fifty thousand Sudanese pounds returned us to square one because our visas were due to expire within one month. By the time I was insolvent in Khartoum with my family, my passport had expired. I had to start everything from the beginning or give up the planned journey or face a new process.

During this time, I had some large expenses and needed funds to cover them. I was not sure how I would cope. This was a time of serious testing and isolation because the local Ngok Lual Yak people in Khartoum were envious of me. Even my cousin Kiir Kon Mamor was under the influence of his new adopted uncle who was so suspicious about offering me help. My young cousin would listen to the advice of his so-called uncle rather than his real blood uncle who was in desperate need and broke. As an example, my cousin Kiir Kon Mamor was given three million Sudanese pounds by the priest of the Church of Christ in Khartoum in order to open his own business. Instead of thinking about my situation with the children in Khartoum, he was encouraged by his adopted uncle to go to Renk right away to buy charcoal there for his small business. Life was consistently challenging and I was feeling like a stranger in my own country with my family. There have been disappointments and frustrations. Those days taught us to exercise patience in many ways. To leave home for such a foreign environment at this stage in life was perhaps one of the greatest challenges a person could undertake and it was certainly not for everyone. I stayed in Khartoum facing the lack of basic living needs for almost two months. Some people amongst my home area were hopeless about my intention because of my financial shortage.

Finally I asked the retired wildlife police Major Deng Giu Gar to give me a loan of two hundred thousand Sudanese pounds in exchange for two cows which he could get in Baliet from my half brother Dol Kiir Lual. I needed the money so desperately for my travel expenses to Egypt with my family. In response to my request, he agreed that he would loan me two hundred thousand Sudanese Pounds and asked me to put this request into writing which I did. The promissory loan request letter was witnessed by his cousin Akol Monyjok Giu and by my maternal uncle Chol Aben Monyjok. Happily, the illiterate old man approved my loan and promised me that he would give me the sum of two hundred thousand Sudanese Pounds within two days. I was completely confident that Mr. Deng Giu Gar would live up his promise and honour his signature. I waited and waited for three weeks instead of two days, hoping that the old man would honour his promise.

Lying is not a part of Dinka society. Indeed it is treated as a curse against those who practice it in Dinka society. Furthermore, lying by a Dinka adult was and is still very rare in the Dinka culture where I was brought up, but it seemed to me that some of the Dinka elders who had been living in Northern Sudan for many years with Arabs turned out to be bigger liars. Before the war interrupted Dinka culture, adults would never tell a lie to the young nor would the young attempt to lie to an adult either.

After I had waited patiently for three weeks to receive the so-called loan, Mr. Deng Giu Gar called me into his room one evening where he was sitting cross-legged in an armchair, surrounded by countless bottles of wine. He had been drinking for the last few weeks. He told me that he was not going to honour my request that he had signed three weeks ago. He said angrily that he had decided to change his mind due to the countless loan requests that he had received from needy individuals. He continued with comments that he was sick of beggars around him which annoyed me indeed. Afterward, the old man angrily scolded people looking for his support, told them to stay away from his place and vowed not to help the poor anymore. I did not know the old man would simply dishonour the commitment he had made to me and embarrassed me. This left me uncertain about what to believe from the Dinka elders who lived in Northern Sudan. I wished I had heeded the advice from the late Monykuc Thon Mabil who advised me earlier that the comfortable old man was just a liar and would not stick to his word. I could not waste my time on an unprofitable deal. But I really thought that the old man was an honest and legitimate gentleman and I thought he was going to give me the money needed for my journey to Egypt. Instead the old man was just lying to me. It was an experience I will never forget.

Chapter 14

PICTURES

With my wife, Aluel and our children in Canada, October 2008

My wife, Aluel and our children

My sons, Kiir (Left) and Lual (Right)

With my children

With my wife, Aluel

My children, Lual (Left),
Arop (Middle) and Kiir (Right)

With my younger son, Lual

With my wife, Aluel

With my two sons,
Kiir (Left) and Lual (Right)

My elder son, Kiir

My younger son, Lual

My wife, Aluel (Left) with my daughter, Arop (Middle) and my son,
Lual (Right)

My brother, Dhieu Kiir Lual (Left)
and Rev. Tor Monybuny Kur
(Right) in Kenya

My mother, Nyanbuny Ayuel
Koryom in Sudan

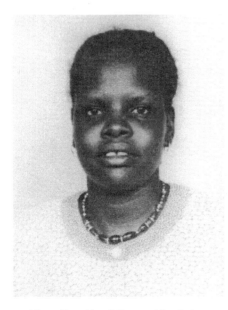

My wife, Aluel Deng Nyok in
Egypt

With my cousin, Magong Dhieu
Kiir (Left) in Sudan, 1998

My brother, Dhieu Kiir Lual
(Right) and Rev. Tor Monybuny
(Left) in Kenya

With my cousin, Pel Kuol
Kong (Behind) and his uncle
Monywac Minyang (Right)
in Sudan

With my friend, Ahol Awan Arop
(Left), my cousins, Akoc Awan Kong
(Behind Left) and nephew, Pul Kuol
Dau (Behind Right)
I'm holding my son, Kiir in Sudan

My brother, Dhieu Kiir Lual (Middle) with his coleagues, politicians
in Malakal, Southern Sudan

135

My late brother,
Kon Mamor Lual

My late brother,
Malik Abiel Lual

My brother, Ranlei Abiel Lual in
Sudan

My photo in Egypt, 2003

My photo during cultural orientation to come to Canada from
Egypt

My cousin, Deng Malik Abiel
in Egypt

With my cousin, Akoc Mirial (Left) and my friend (Right) in Egypt,
2003

With Koryom Kur Monyluak (Left) and Nyandeng Paduom Ayuel
(Right) in Egypt, 2003

With my cousin, Deng Malik Abiel in the airport of Egypt,
on October 28th, 2003

With my late friend, Abiel Deng
Thon (Left) in Egypt, 2003

With Thon Bol Biliu (Left)
in Egypt, 2003

My brother, Dhieu Kiir Lual (Right) sharing a hug with
Dr. Lam Akol Ajakwin (Left) in Malakal

My brother, Dhieu Kiir Lual speaking in Baliet county headquaters, during his tenure as commissioner of Baliet county in 2006, Sudan

Shortly after my confirmation at the Mount Zion Lutheran Church in New Westminster, BC on May 30th, 2004

With my brother in law, Luat Magai (Right) and Lual Atok (Left) and Nyanguek (Sitting)

With Kat Tiop Lual (Left), Nyandeng Paduom Ayuel (Right) and Koryom Kur Monyluak (Far Right)

With Luat (Sitting Left) and Monyror Kuany (Sitting Right) and other friends in Egypt

141

With my cousin Akoc Mirial (Far Left), Hakim Akuol Deng (Left) and Koryom Kur Monyluak (Right)

With my friends in Egypt during my farewell prayer in October, 2003

With my friend, Deng Mabil (Left), Achuei Mijak, Akuol Kual,
my wife, Aluel, and Nyanbol Nyok Malith (to the Right)
in the first week in Canada

With my elder son, Kiir (Middle Left), my friend, Deng Mabil
(Middle Right), and my wife, Aluel (Right)

With my friends, Agei Malek (Left), Akok Manyang (Right)
and Herpa Kejela (Far Right)

With my friends, Akok Manyang (Left), Akok Deng (Right)
and Agei Malek (Far Right)

With my friends, Trilby McGaw (Middle), Akok Manyang (Right)
in Vancouver, BC

With my friends, Trilby McGaw (Left), Akok Manyang (Middle)
in Vancouver, BC

At the farewell prayer at St. Andrew United Church in Egypt
before coming to Canada, 2003

Chapter 15

HAUNTING HUMILIATION IN KHARTOUM

Many people from my own community of Ngok Lual Yak started to label me as a mere beggar without any goals. They soon began to humiliate me although some were aware of my situation in Khartoum. Of those individuals who had left Southern Sudan before the civil war broke out in 1983, most had never endured the hardships as I had for some years. They were enjoying their lives in the squatter camps around Khartoum, which they were proud to call home. These individuals kept beating their drum of my suffering through many ways to discourage me and my family from our planned journey to Egypt.

In a week, things soon turned sour because my fellow brother from Ajuba area, Mr. Abraham Nyok Aguek, who used to be the owner of the restaurant in Khartoum felt jealous about my staying in his house with my family. Instead of telling me the truth as a Dinka man, he hid his feelings from me and told a gathering of his workers and servants in his restaurant that his house had been overcrowded by my family whom he believed were evading starvation in Kenana. His servants laughed disapprovingly, but one of my acquaintances who were around during this gathering came and told this "funny joke" to me. I was so shocked at what he said against me and my family. I could not eat any food that evening in his house. I just had my bath, spread my mat on the floor and went to sleep. How did he expect me to be able to eat in his house after such humiliation? But it was a word that was quickly taken up by other members of the Ngok Lual Yak community members, including my maternal Uncle Chol Aben Monyjok. In Khartoum people were started to give me the nickname of a homeless man. One day, we noticed that two men and a woman were laughing at us and we joined in their fun by telling them that we were here in Khartoum with the worthy goal of going to Egypt, but we were not beggars. We were the only poor people in the community, but we did not feel any embarrassment. The businessman thought we had fled the starvation zone in Kenana, as he called it, to come to Khartoum to fill up our empty stomachs with the leftover rare dinners in his house which he said was like a feeding centre. I began to question why I went to his house because there was no reason to go there while my maternal uncle Chol Aben Monyjok was in Khartoum. I had never met such merciless people who, despite having enough to share, are so selfish and grumpy. Needless to say, it was an experience I will take with me for the rest of my life.

In anger I wrapped up my few bags which contained almost nothing and moved my family to the house of my maternal uncle Chol Aben Monyjok. I was warmly welcomed with my family by my cousin Akoc Mirial Kuol in the house of the man whom I thought would be helpful. Little did I know that I would be treated like an outcast in the house of my own maternal uncle Chol Aben Monyjok? At that time my uncle Chol Aben Monyjok was at his job in Helig in Western Upper Nile State where he was working with a Canadian Oil Company. I thought I would be free from insults with my family if I lived in the house of my own maternal uncle Chol Aben Monyjok. But it was the beginning of my humiliations with my family and I accepted it on the condition that we were homeless. After nine days my uncle Chol Aben Monyjok returned to Khartoum. Soon after his arrival, his self-declared friend Akol Monyjok Giu did not give him time to interact with me because he was against my receiving assistance. He kept flattering me that he was very concerned about my situation, but in reality he was kidding, though he was not sure that I was aware of his reluctance. My maternal uncle Chol Aben Monyjok was the person I hoped would help me to cover the costs of my travel tickets to Egypt. Instead of helping me, he flatly refused even to assist my little children who just required something to eat, not money for tickets. A few days later, I broached the subject of money to him, and I was extremely sorry when he tried to wriggle out of it. I had a discussion with him for days trying to convince him to give me some financial support. In response, he tried to convince me to give up my trip to Egypt saying that my travel was full of temptations because he was greatly influenced by his close friend and relied heavily on his suggestions and advice. As a result he advised me to pack up and go to my mother in Southern Sudan because he said it was no use wasting money and resources on an unsuccessful emigration process. When I refused his advice, he lost his patience with me right away. I will never forget his reaction and response. He looked at me as if I had insulted him and went to Malakal to see his family whom he thought was free from bad luck.

LIFE IN DIRE NEED OF FINANCIAL STRAITS

He left me with my family in dire financial straits. This showed me how tricky it is to solve your financial problems by relying on individual support even, if that support is from your own brother. I remained penniless in his house but equipped with hope that I was going to succeed, and that certainly helped. My maternal uncle Chol Aben Monyjok urged me to listen to his advice and go to South Sudan or face starvation in Khartoum, but I refused his first suggestion and faced the hunger instead. Being in a city like Khartoum without enough money to subsist on was difficult for a stranger like me, because it was my second time in Khartoum and I did not know the city very well. To earn our daily bread, my wife was working as a dishwasher in the homes of Arab women in Khartoum while I was busily visiting the Humanitarian Aid Office in Khartoum to seek some financial support. To make life even more difficult, my son Kiir became very sick. He would cry and run in horror as he saw his own shadow at night. We endured this test until I took him to the health centre where the Arab doctor took the little money we had as examination fees. Then, he sent us away with our sick son without a written prescription for medicine to treat our son. We were only left with hope but no money in our pocket or food.

After one month, my maternal uncle Chol Aben Monyjok came back from Malakal with the hope that I would hear his advice to give up going to Egypt but I did not want to hear such advice. He kept suggesting that I should go back to Baliet in Southern Sudan where my mother was living so she could take me to the local magicians for my bad luck. Meanwhile his friends were suggesting that I go to the bush to join the SPLA rebel movement as a volunteer freedom fighter instead. These people thought it was more worthy to be a soldier than anything else because they were thinking that I was not fit to go to abroad like their in-laws and relatives. My worth, according to these individuals, was to join the rebels in the SPLA movement as a volunteer fighter while they were enjoying the comforts of city life with their families and relatives. These pitiless people maintained they were faithful Christians, but their selfishness and manners toward the less fortune spoke otherwise. Both individuals were reluctant about encouraging our children for further studies because they might compete with their children, who were gaining a lucrative education in private schools unlike our children who were living from hand to mouth. According to their thoughts, they were the ones who wanted their children to go to school and discouraged the rest of the children from going to school so that they would become cattle herders and remain illiterate. One Saturday evening in Khartoum, two friends of my maternal uncle Chol Aben Monyjok were joking against me while he was around, but, instead of helping me, he hurled abuse at me and praised his bloating friends for their efforts to humiliate me. Then the next evening my maternal uncle Chol Aben Monyjok came to me while I was joking with my nephew Riak Deng Chan and asked me why my wife was working as a cleaner in the home of the Arab women in Khartoum while I was sitting there. When I patiently told my maternal uncle that we were penniless, he broke into derisive laughter as I continued to explain to him that we were in a situation where my wife and I were partners, and that the work of either one of us would make a difference to stabilize our dire financial situations. He made another rude comment that did not justify an answer. I permitted him to go because there was nothing to be gained from getting into the argument he wanted, and I was not going to let one madcap mess up what had been a very tough experience with selfish people. The comfortable man just laughed loudly and said that his wife would not work as a servant in the houses of Arab women like my wife as long as he was still alive. After his pessimistic conversation with me, he hurriedly returned back to the house of his friend Akol Monyjok Giu to enjoy more laughter over coffee. The man had been in disagreement with me on the issue of my journey yet I did not renounce him as flawed because he was a crazy but lovable uncle, even though he was humiliating me with his best friend. From then on, the men were looking for every opportunity to make things difficult for me and my family. Day after day I had to endure insults from people, most of whom I would call my own people, and my maternal uncle Chol Aben Monyjok did nothing but follow suit.

When my maternal uncle Chol Aben started attending school, my mother was the one who used to hold him by the hand every day to and from school, not to mention the insults she had to endure because she dared to keep him from the bullies. Now he had turned his back on me and simply forgot the kind assistance my mother had given to him during his childhood. Despite my ignoring their insults, these people made a lot of fun of me as if I had a tail. They started to give me several names, ranging from homeless man, greedy, and father of shoeless children. In addition, I was also called the husband of the dishwasher woman while my children were treated like outcasts. But all these names and insults did not deter me from my planned journey, nor did they discourage me in many ways as was expected by these self declared rich men. They made fun of me all the time, even though they were my own relatives and members of my clan. My maternal uncle Chol Aben and his cronies were treating me like an outcast because I did not agree with their advice to give up on my journey to Egypt. The merciless groups were proposing that it was their in-laws who deserved to go abroad to benefit from the luxuries of life in Western countries and wanted me to go to the bush to join the rebels as a volunteer fighter. They would joke against me and my family until the middle of the night because I did not respect their advice.

My wife Aluel Deng Nyok once complained about these names to me and I told her not to mind them. I kept reassuring my children and my wife that the hardship was temporary and that our family would get through it and everything would be fine in the near future.

The forty seven days of my stay in Khartoum with my family were tough because many members of my community thought I was at their doors to ask for money and food. This embarrassed me and my wife who used to accompany me. The many insults that I endured pressured me to make the decision to miss quite a few evening meals with these heartless people and quietly go hungry. I thought that if I missed some evening meals without eating with these compassionless individuals, then it might decrease my evening insults. I thought it was a good choice but I was not aware that I was just abusing myself. Steadily, I became so weak from hunger and I lost more than six pounds from my already thin frame. After fasting for four days, I was almost starving and I collapsed from hunger on the sidewalk in Khartoum. A passerby rushed to my aid and took me to the hospital in Khartoum where I was later told by the doctor that my collapse was caused by hunger. The doctor ordered the nurse to provide me with food as my treatment in the hospital, something I regretted when I was discharged after six hours. Before I was discharged the doctor suggested that I should eat three times a day, something which I could not afford during those days in Khartoum. At that time, six thousand Sudanese pounds ensured that a family of four could eat nutritiously for three meals per day, an unaffordable amount for a man who was penniless. I felt really bad about this incident and I went home late at night after I was discharged from the hospital. When I arrived at the house my wife asked me where I had been and I told her that I was in the house of my former classmate. I did not reveal this incident to my wife until I came to Canada. Had I told my wife about this episode, she would have forced the cancellation of our journey to Egypt for fear of starvation. Despite this hardship my wife Aluel Deng Nyok was always by my side, never losing her self-control even when thing kept going badly.

My devoted wife has been a constant source of support to me through all the difficulties that we faced in our journey. We attempted our level best and achieved our financial goals despite the lengthy insults from these individuals amongst our community in Khartoum who were envious of us and were attempting to discourage us through many tests.

FINDING HELP FROM FINANCIAL DESPERATION

Just three weeks after my maternal Uncle Chol Aben had left me broke and penniless in his house, I was given a loan by Thon Kur Monyluak. This man came to me one day and asked me about the progress of my immigration process for Egypt. I told him I was short of money and that was why I was still hanging around Khartoum. He asked me how much money I needed to cover my travel expenses and I told him I needed two hundred thousand Sudanese pounds. Then he told me that he had a friend who would give me two hundred thousand Sudanese pounds in exchange for two cows. He agreed to let me borrow the money in return for which I would give him a fixed proportion of the profits of every cow. I agreed with him right away. After that I wrote a letter and attached a recorded voice cassette as confirmation to my half brother Dol Kiir Lual to hand over the two conceived heifers to Thon Kur Monyluak without any further delays in exchange for the loan he had given me. Since the market price of the cows had soared to five hundred thousand Sudanese Pounds each in Malakal, it was a bargain which was obtained in difficulty, but the support that Thon Kur Monyluak provided was vital for the success of my travel plans. I credited the success of this loan negotiation to my nephew Riak Deng Chan who convinced his half brother Thon Kur Monyluak to give me the loan. Mr. Gak Tuong Deng also played a role in securing my loan because he accompanied me to the house of Thon Kur Monyluak. In addition, Mr Gak Tuong Deng told Thon Kur Monyluak about my needs and offered to sign the letter of the loan as one of the witnesses with my nephew Riak Deng Chan.

These gentlemen helped me greatly to secure my loan and I shall not forget their support.

Soon after I received the loan I went to the Ministry of Interior Affairs to get our exit visas, but the Immigration Officer in charge of the exit visas told me to renew my passport instead. This confused me but I resolved to renew it without any hesitation. My passport would have expired four months later, but the Immigration Officer just wanted me to spend the money I had in my pocket so I could not go to Egypt. Before I renewed my passport, I tried to persuade the Immigration Officer to issue my visa but he refused and told me to go away from his office because the Immigration Officials were not pleased to see people from Southern Sudan go to Egypt. They were used to overcharging our fees as if we were not Sudanese citizens when we obtained our travel documents from them.

After I got the loan from Thon Kur Monyluak, I was scheduled to go on Monday, April 2, 2002. My maternal uncle Chol Aben Monyjok almost fainted after he had heard that I had the money and would leave for Egypt on Monday. When my nephew Riak Deng Chan returned home that evening, he communicated this good news to my maternal uncle Chol Aben Monyjok and his friend Akol Monyjok Giu but neither of them appeared particularly delighted. Instead they shouted loudly in Dinka language: "engo jo raan piou dit ele" which means "Why is this person so greedy like that?" The next morning, the news of my loan were spread to the entire Ngok Lual Yak community in Khartoum. The homeless man had found himself a loan at last, people said throughout Khartoum, and they started to look at me as the crow flies, as if I had suddenly grown wings. They never thought I would get enough support to go to Egypt. After forty-seven days in Khartoum, which sometimes brought moments of depression, I was able to leave Sudan for Egypt. During this time I never once stood still and gave up on my goal. In fact it only gave me more energy to persevere and achieve success in my journey to Egypt. After enduring the looks and taunts of those who were opposing my process and facing hardships in Khartoum, I got what I was looking for and on April 2, 2002, as scheduled, I was able to leave Sudan for Egypt with my family.

Chagai Chol Lual

Chapter 16

FROM SUDAN TO EGYPT BY TRAIN AND FERRY

We left the house of my maternal uncle Chol Aben Monyjok in the early morning at about 5: oo a.m. We were taken to the railway station by taxi and were accompanied to the railway station by Mr. Aguek Deng Dak, because my maternal uncle Chol Aben Monyjok was too shy about what to do and excused himself by pretending that he was sick and unable to accompany us to the railway station. As we boarded our train at 7:30 a.m we waved farewell to Mr. Aguek Deng Dak. Then the train left the station as scheduled at 8:30 a.m. I heard the clang of the iron bumpers and felt the gentle pull as the train began to move. The train began to roll faster and then we were off to Wadi-halfa on April 2, 2002. It was a gruelling two-days-long train trip to Wadi-Halfa where we were transported like cattle in a railway train. My sons were very excited with the train ride while I was terrified and fearful. It was my first train ride and I was not comfortable with it. All of us had left relatives and friends behind with no assurance of ever seeing them again. In addition, I was aware of my elderly mother and my three siblings. The train attendants provided bread sandwiches for dinner. We ate them with our children even though the sandwiches were tasteless and managed the rest of our bread carefully so that they would last for the duration of the trip. We arrived in Wad-Halfa on April 3, 2002 in the evening and headed to the Nile Hotel that was beside the river. The hotel was like a prison because there was neither light nor heat. We spent the night fighting the cold. The next evening we boarded the ferryboat for Egypt and arrived in Egypt through the port of Aswan on April 4, 2002. Shortly after our arrival we took a microbus from Aswan to Cairo. The journey was free because the microbus driver wanted to use our passports to buy goods from the duty-free shops in Cairo. Before we took off for Cairo the microbus driver took our passports. I was not happy with this driver for keeping our passport with him. However, he insisted that it was the system, the way things were done in Egypt and he showed me the passports he had in the drawer of his car. I simply nodded my head and handed over our passports to him. I never liked the idea of parting with my passport after my experience in Khartoum when a thief tricked me and took my passport with some cash. After a long, boring ride, we arrived in Cairo, shabbily dressed and in torn shoes. The driver took us to the Sacred Heart Catholic Church in Cairo in Egypt.

We spent four hours waiting in the church because our microbus driver was buying goods from the duty-free shops with our passports. Despite the delay, my brother in-law, Luat Magai Lueth, was there, waiting to pick us up in the church. I smiled when I saw him for the first time in three years. We hugged. "Welcome to Egypt," he said. After we received our passports, we were taken by Luat Magai Lueth to their rented apartment where most of our community members were staying, including my brother-in-law Luat Magai. Two hours later my cousin, Deng Malik Abiel, who was in Egypt learned about my arrival from Koryom Kur Monyluak, better known by his imposed nickname as chief of Ajuba. My cousin Deng Malik Abiel came to the house where we were staying. We were really tired and weak from hunger which was evident in our eyes. Shortly after our arrival Mr. Guil Amol Guil brought us our first Egyptian meal which was totally different from our home food in Sudan. We ate it slowly like bride. Guil Amol Guil was one of the few generous men I have ever found in Ngok Lual Yak community. I will never forget his generousity and caring. After we ate we were directed to a room where we slept well with stomachs that have not been so full with food for nearly one week or more. While we were still asleep, my cousin Deng Malik Abiel comes back and forth to bring our luggage to his apartment. He came back again to wait for us until we were awake and then took us to his rental room to stay with him. He gave us his room and offered to sleep on the floor in the living room because I was his paternal uncle. Our situation changed dramatically because we were offered help right away. Mr. Luat Magai Lueth, who is currently residing in Israel, provided us with clothes and money for several months to rebuild our lives while Mr. Hakim Kuol Deng brought us clothes and also provided countless financial support. I owed a lot to these two gentlemen for supporting us financially until the time when we could get back on our feet in Egypt.

We stayed with my cousin Deng Malik Abiel for one month until we finally settled in the city of Cairo where we shared the rent of two bedrooms with my friend Mr. Thon Deng Chol Maluth and his family as roommates. We just needed roof over our heads, not a good house with everything because there was no television or telephone line. Eventually Mr. Thon Maluth and his family left Egypt for Australia. They told us of the good life and countless opportunities in Australia and wished we were present to rebuild our lives together. We continued to remain in this apartment. We never had any phone number by which we could have been reached regarding the status of our resettlement programs from the office of the United Nations High Commissioner for Refugee in Cairo. After Thon Maluth and his family left, we were joined by Mr. Monyror Kuany Monyluak, his children, and his wonderful wife Amou Monybuny Kur, who later moved to America in 2004 where they are now residing. When I was in Egypt, after many years of absence, I began to go to church every Sunday at Saint Andrew United Church in Cairo.

On April 6, 2002, I went to the office of the United Nations High Commissioner for Refugees in Egypt with my cousin Deng, to register for refugee asylum. During the time for the preparation of our case history for refugee status we were given a helping hand by the foreign sister named Claire Darwin, a generous white woman with a gracious gift from England. Mr.Thon Bol Biliu was able to volunteer his time to help me with this young white lady in the completion of my case history prior to my interview with the UN staff in Egypt. It was the most wonderful support I had ever received from foreigner and after she left for England, I burst into tears wondering how foreigners could be so caring to people they did not even know. I knew then that love came from God but I kept on being surprised. I owe a lot to Thon Bol Biliu for helping me during the writing of my case history and I will never forget his help with Claire Darwin in Egypt.

We were interviewed by the UNHCR staff for our refugee status on September 17, 2002 in Cairo in Egypt. Our interview lasted for five hours and we were recognized as refugees by the United Nations High Commissioner for Refugee (UNHCR) on December 12, 2002. After three months, we were transferred to the Canadian Consulate in Cairo in Egypt for a resettlement program in Canada.

The Egyptians were terrifying people and the deportation of Sudanese refugees back to Sudan was a usual occurrence. The risks in daily living were high. Sometimes the Egyptian police would arrested the Sudanese and deport them back to Sudan. My wife was working as janitor in the morning to earn some money while I looked after our two children and worked part-time cleaning a restaurant in the evenings to supplement our bare-bones budget. We worked like this until our refugee status was settled. I had an ambition to study, but for the time being, all I could think of was to work hard to pay for our rent and food.

REFUGEE WITHOUT HEALTH INSURANCE

When my son Kiir was born in 1997 he was an attractive baby boy who was healthy and cute. Our cheerfulness knew no bounds as we lived in the Kenana industrial area and life was wonderful. On March 18, 2003, my son become very sick and ended up in hospital in Cairo in Egypt. When Kiir was sick in Egypt our world seemed to fall apart. He had not been well for some time, so I took him to the hospital. I will never forget the moment when the doctor told me that my son was suffering from an allergy in his heart that caused him to cough recurrently. This was one of the life-threatening sicknesses that my son contracted six years after his birth. It was hard to grapple with the thought that our little boy was stricken with a fearsome allergic reaction in his heart. He had just started to become aware of the world around him and now he was fighting for his life. The doctor said that a very successful medical treatment might be administered, consisting of ultrasound and numerous health check-ups. This was our next surprise. We definitely loved our son and wanted the best medical care for him. The doctor transferred my son Kiir to the hospital that partnered with the United Nations High Commissioner for Refugees in Cairo for further treatment. As soon as we met the doctor at the hospital, I was once more calmed. The doctor was very sympathetic and guaranteed me that he would do everything possible to treat my son Kiir without the registration fee. I felt thankful to see that even in a foreign country we had those who were standing by our side. After four days Kiir's health was worsening and he was soon transferred to another hospital to see a chest specialist. He was admitted to that hospital right away on March 18, 2003 where he was given the oxygen ventilator to help him to breathe. The doctor put him on oxygen and hooked him up to an intravenous line and monitors. He remained in intensive care for three days. In the following days, he continued to improve. Now the question was: how are we going to pay for the treatment of our son? We were surprised that the two months of treatments for our son Kiir would cost about five thousand Egyptian pounds. We did not have anywhere near that much money and yet it was essential to start the treatment of our son at once. Having left Sudan for Egypt as refugees, we were not entitled to any open health insurance. Hence, we were with our extremely sick son who was in desperate need of medical attention. Medical expertise was ready to lend a hand to treat our son, but we did not have enough funds. However, the doctor came to our rescue and told us that the treatments could start right away if we made down payment of three thousand Egyptian pounds and signed a guarantee for the rest. We had some savings and with help from our friends, we were able to pay the down payment of three thousand Egyptian pounds and promised to pay the rest through instalments. But it was expensive to maintain him there even though a number of friends and acquaintances contributed their pittance to his upkeep each day. During that time it was very difficult and exhausting both for our son and for us. On the other hand, we were in high spirits and grateful as our son showed signs of improvement. He started to breathe on his own without the help of the oxygen ventilator. As a result, he spent three days in hospital but his coughing lasted for two months. After three months, the ultrasound performed on his chest showed no traces of allergic reaction in his heart. Six months later, he improved totally to our own surprise and that of the doctors and he is now a joyful boy without any sign of allergic reactions in his heart.

The day Kiir was discharged from the hospital was the day after the day that American troops had attacked Iraq and the Egyptian public was protesting throughout the entire country. Despite police warnings, thousand of Egyptian Muslims mobbed the streets and bus stations in Cairo in order to attack, to beat up, or stone to death any foreigners that they might get hold of in those streets because they were upset about the attack on Iraq. However, Kiir and I did not know that Iraq had been attacked the previous night by the American troops, so we were the only foreigners on the bus amongst the Egyptian people, some of whom were hunting for foreigners to stone to death. When I arrived in the house, people started to pray God including my wife, about our safe arrival because they knew that the Egyptian Muslims were stoning foreigners in the streets. I too was grateful to God for my safety and that of my son Kiir.

FLIGHT TO CANADA WITH JOY AND FRIGHT

After seventeen months in Egypt, I was accepted for re-settlement in Canada with my family. When I first climbed into the airplane on October 28, 2003 in Cairo International Airport, the plane was an adventure for my family and it was a scare for me personally. It certainly did not look like the safest form of transportation to me. In spite of some safety concerns, I climbed in the backseat with my family and nervously bucked our seat-belts after we were shown how to buckle our lap belts by the flight attendant. The pilot, obliviously to my anxiety, secured the plane and sped full steam down the runway for take-off. Once safely in the air, I forced myself to calm down. It was my first airplane ride and I was so nervous that I wanted the ground to open and swallow me. Truly, I did not know much about planes and I feared we might fall into the ocean. As such, I was actually frightened in the plane for several hours. Little did we know that this incredible trip would be only of many that awaited us once we arrived in Canada?

We flew first to Germany with other refugees on board. When the plane hit the ground in Frankfurt Airport for a stop-over, the passengers expressed their joy. After stepping off the plane, we made our way to another gate and proceeded to wait for our flight to Canada inside the airport in Germany where teams of friendly but strict officials were guiding us efficiently to pass the Red Cross passports and International Organization for Migration (IOM) bags at the customs checkpoints. We were exhausted and hungry as we waited but there was nothing to fill our hungry mouths as we were just penniless refugees. After a four-hour stopover we then boarded an airplane that flew us to Vancouver in Canada.

Further to the countless wonders was the terrifying force of the confused winds that tossed our plane up and down for about an hour. That was worse than any amusement or bumpy road ride I have ever been on. Being a cattle man from a remote area, I had never been on a plane before and I was extremely worried but it was certainly fun. Then my son Kiir asked me to take him to the washroom, but I simply told my son that there was no washroom on this plane. Of course I was very nervous and I did not want to walk inside the plane for fear that I would fall down and hurt myself. The boy looked straight at me as if he already knew that there might be a washroom somewhere in the plane. After a few minutes, my son got up and walked around by himself in the plane and found the washroom. Before he had moved further, I told him not to wander in the plane in case he would get lost, something my son still wonders about to this day. After all how anyone could get lost in an airplane, just as how could an airplane have no washroom in it? When my son returned to his seat he was just smiling and told me that he had found the washroom and that he would be happy to show me where the washroom was located. Well, I told my son to take me to the washroom which he did. My son led me like a blind man on board in order to show me the washroom because he understood his father was nervous, although he did not tell me directly.   It was a flight I will never forget, and I have never been more proud of my son and his loving efforts to help me on board. Today I can laugh about the ordeal with my son.

Chapter 17

ARRIVING IN CANADA TO REBUILD OUR LIVES

After a gruelling flight of nine hours from Germany, we arrived at Vancouver International Airport in Canada as landed immigrants at about 4:30 pm on October 28, 2003. Suddenly, the plane rose sharply and we were all startled by a terrible noise from below. The pilot announced our welcome to Canada and assured us that the plane had arrived in Vancouver International Airport. In reality, we thought that our journey to Canada from Egypt might have taken us four days.

Shortly after our arrival, we exited the plane and felt the Canadian cold engulf us like ice. We were without jackets and were shocked by the freezing cold that slashed our bare faces and hands. We were really freezing before the Immigration staff gave us some warm clothes in the Airport. Upon departing the plane in Vancouver International Airport, we found ourselves by a huge number of new sights. Several things that Canadians take for granted both scared us, especially the moving staircase that seemed to magically transport us from up to down, making it appear as if we were floating through the air. I had an awful experience on such staircase because when I stepped to it, it moved abruptly and I screamed in fear as I began to fall forward. Had the Immigration Officer behind me did not grabbed my arms and pulled me back to safety, the staircase would have knocked me over and I would have truly hurt myself that day from the fall.

After clearing Immigration and Customs, we sat pitifully near our luggage, not sure about where we should go until we were driven by taxi from the Airport to the Welcome House reception centre run by the Immigrant Services Society of British Columbia. We were warmly received by the Immigrant Service Society Staff who gave us some money and a cultural orientation the next morning. My son Kiir was very airsick upon our arrival in Canada. His coughing degenerated massively as we arrived in the Welcome House Reception Centre. Shortly after our arrival in Vancouver, I had no idea how I was going to continue my life with my family in this new land, coupled with the fact that I knew nobody here in Vancouver. It took deep faith and a lot of patience to get used to.

After two days, I met the future Sudanese journalist Mading Ngor Akec who is now studying journalism at the University of Edmonton in Alberta. Amazingly, Mading Ngor Akec was from Dinka Bor and I was from Dinka Padang but we were all from the Dinka tribe. However, we were able to understand one another despite language variation beween the two Dinka communities. Mr. Mading Ngor Akec volunteered to help me take my sick son to the Mount Saint Joseph Hospital in Vancouver to see a doctor who could help my son but we also got lost that day and had a hard time finding our way back to the Welcome House Reception Centre. Finally, we gave up finding the hospital and returned back without any treatment to lessen the massive coughing of my son. We spent two frightening weeks having medical tests and orientations in the Welcome House Reception Centre before we moved to our rented apartment in Burnaby.

To be honest, we experienced culture shock in our first weeks of stay on the foreign soil in the Welcome House Reception Centre. Automatic doors were amazing things, let alone the SkyTrain ride. When we entered into the elevator, we were completely confused about what to do. When the elevator went down, we ran around in horror like frantic cats. But when the elevator went up, we would attempt to grasp onto anything we could seize. One newly-arrived immigrant woman went to the bathroom to take the shower. Once she attempted to turn on the water hose on herself and mistakenly turned the hot water on her nude body. She fled the bathroom purely naked to the living room where we were sitting and murmured some words that we did not understood.

Soon after our arrival, I also met Mayich Kuch Makuac in the Welcome House Reception Centre where he was staying with his family since his arrival from Egypt two weeks earlier.

Even though, Mayich was a Sudanese refugee in Egypt, we had never seen one another before, but we were able to make solid friendships in an unbelievably short period of time. After four days in the Welcome House reception centre, I met Deng Akec Manyuon Biar better known as Deng Biar and we quickly got to know one another through joking. Right away we felt like old friends. To this day, Mayich Makuac and Deng Biar with their families have become our close family friends in North America. After one week in the Welcome House, we were invited by Yai Lual Nuer and his generous wife Nyanut Akol Tong who arranged a dinner in our honour in their home in New Westminster. After almost three weeks in Welcome House, we moved to our rented apartment in Burnaby. We received financial assistance from the Canadian Government for one year.

WRENCHING CULTURAL ADJUSTMENT IN CANADA

After our arrival in Canada we felt that we were thrown into a very strange and different world and had to learn how to become comfortable and familiar with a new way of living. It was sort of cultural shock in the modern society on our first day in the foreign soil. The whole thing was really different from our expectations in the country where freedom was like breathing. We were told during the orientation session that household tasks, including cooking, are a normal shared task between a husband and wife in North America. The new immigrants raised their concerns about those couples who were coming from Africa or the Middle East where men do not cook nor sit near the kitchen. Nobody bothered to answer this question anyway. As I have mentioned, the cooking issue was something that I thought would never cross my path again after what I had endured in the refugee camp in Ethiopia. I thought I had my own wife who would take care of cooking but that is not the case in North America where everyone shares household duties. As newcomers we struggled to figure out how to use a vacuum cleaner. When it came time for cooking, I was the first person to grab the clothes and rush them to the laundry and then pick up the vacuum to vacuum the whole area in our home, including the living room. My wife would smile before she would take the rest of the jobs, like cooking, and our family enjoyed the meal together. To me it seems that the family structure in western world treasures the women as heads of the families and decision makers, followed by their children while the husbands are the least powerless people in their families to have a say. The majority of the immigrant women who came from Third World countries where men lead them like blind persons for many years took advantage of this freedom as a golden chance to kick out their long-time husbands in their homes with the help of the police. Then they would simply replace their husbands with so-called boy friends. This thing left the immigrant men uncertain about the countries they thought would be helpful to achieve their dream of raising up their own families without instigating family violence. However, after surviving as the new immigrants, we settled in Canada and embraced the opportunity to learn about the dissimilar life and culture from the ones we were accustomed to in Africa.

Two months after our arrival in Canada, I immediately went to Mount Zion Lutheran Church in New Westminster in British Columbia with my family. Later, I joined the membership confirmation class to refresh myself and I was confirmed at Mount Zion Lutheran Church in New Westminster in British Columbia and I sat on Church council for two terms. Above all, I have learned what it means to be a Lutheran and it was very stimulating and enjoyable for me. Afterward, I made rapid spiritual progress and this warmed my heart and helped me to get adjusted to this new environment. In addition, I was blessed to meet Rev. Marlys Moen who had a huge heart for the people of Africa.

After one year in Canada, I got employment in various companies. I understood the hardships that the refugee immigrants faced because when I came to Canada I was penniless and struggling to learn English. I had taken English in school for almost ten years in both Ethiopia and Sudan but I was far from being fluent in English and I decided to improve my education. Since learning was the thing I enjoyed most, my ambition to pursue a career in the field of administration had always been a part of my plan since I studies at college in Sudan. I never wanted to be an accountant because I hated the math and I did not want a career that just focused on numbers. I wanted something more exciting than accounting and that is why I chose management. But a college course in Canada was a long way off for someone who comes from Third World countries like me. It took me nearly two years just to meet the entry qualification and I earned my diploma in management in Canada from the Vancouver Career College in 2005. My early days at the college were not easy. The lecture auditorium was commonly filled with about two hundred students, mostly immigrants who were not born in Canada, many of whom gave up the course within a few weeks. I was strong-minded not to give up but to follow through on what I had started. Moreover, I credited my wife Aluel for being able to support me. She gave me the freedom to go and pursue my dreams though she supported me during all these times. I do not think I will ever be able to repay her in my lifetime, but I am doing my best.

TURNING MY CHILDHOOD DREAM INTO REALITY

I have always been interested in helping deprived people, even though I may have been too young to realize it at the time. From my earliest youth, I had a compassionate heart and I felt a passionate desire for helping the less fortunate around me and beyond. I was the compassionate boy in the village and I used to share my little food with other boys in my area. In addition, I used to visit the sick people in the entire area and then I would help the blind people in the Ajuba area. I would lead the blind elders via sticks to and from their homes to the gathering place where they could share jokes. As a child, I dreamed that one day I would help the orphans and homeless children to give them hope and a future. God might have planted the mission in my heart that has continued to grip me and I guarantee that no matter how long it takes I will accomplish my dreams.

Since I have the heart to help others, I was able to establish the Padang Lutheran Christian Relief in 2005 with the goal of helping the deprived children in Sudan. I know what it is like to go hungry after all my unpleasant life experiences. No matter how pronounced my tiredness, one of my most consistently taxing ordeals in my childhood was to go without food. I disliked this most of all. First I was told by some of my friends that I was letting my talent to waste, but I realized that any achievement is a worthwhile. Being in the refugee camps for years in Ethiopia and Egypt has further fuelled my childhood desire to help those most in need in Africa, especially destitute refugees who have nowhere to stay warm except the board tents where refugees live without employment. Through many hardships, I learned that impossible is only an estimation. One of the biggest dreams of my life was to build orphanages, a school and a hospital in Southern Sudan because I have never forgotten about the suffering of those orphans in Sudan who have no orphanages and schools. Even though I am struggling to raise my own family with my modest income, I have spent twenty percent of my own income for mailing funding proposals and fundraising activities for the sake of others. Currently, I am overseeing the operation of the Padang Lutheran Christian Relief. I often postponed my sleep in order to accomplish this mission. My wife Aluel provided home daycare for two children as well as our own three children to help meet expenses.

My mother said she would be happy to see me helping others before she dies. My plan is to go to South Sudan in early 2009 to begin laying the groundwork for building a school in Baliet County. I plan to stay in South Sudan for two months which means being away from my wife and children for a long time. But that is okay because I will be helping those who would otherwise have no help or hope. My childhood hardships truly have helped to prepare me for life!

ABOUT THE AUTHOR

Chagai Chol Lual was born in 1972 and grew up in Ajuba farming community in Baliet County of Upper Nile State in Southern Sudan. In 1987 when civil war came to his peaceful village, he fled on foot to Ethiopia and spent five years in the Refugee Camp in Ethiopia. Later, the Ethiopian rebels expelled him back to the war zone in Southern Sudan in 1991 along with countless Sudanese refugees.

In 2002, Mr. Chagai Lual immigrated to Egypt with his family and eventually came to Canada in October 2003 with his family as government assisted refugees.

Mr. Chagai Lual is now a Canadian citizen and lives in Vancouver, Canada with his wife and three children.

In addition to writing, Mr. Chagai Lual is the founder and Executive Director of Padang Lutheran Christian Relief, an organization he established in 2005 to provide relief to the most destitute of the returnees and refugees in Southern Sudan.

ISBN 978-142690147-8